If David Shibley had been l̶ ̶ ̶ ̶ ̶ ̶ ̶ ̶ ̶ ̶ ̶ ̶ ̶ ̶ be in every "History's Missionary Heroes" book today. That's why we need to listen to him *now*—he's a voice to our generation for effective missionary enterprise as history is being made today.

—JACK W. HAYFORD, FOUNDING PASTOR/CHANCELLOR
THE CHURCH ON THE WAY/THE KING'S COLLEGE AND SEMINARY

We are living in a day when the Spirit is speaking strongly to the churches about radical new wineskins. No one I know is hearing from the Holy Spirit more clearly about the new missions wineskin than my friend David Shibley. I urge everyone who wants to be on the cutting edge of what God is doing today to read and digest *The Missions Addiction.*

—C. PETER WAGNER, CHANCELLOR
WAGNER LEADERSHIP INSTITUTE

I have known David Shibley since he was a lad. His integrity is unquestioned, and his ministry is international. He is a trusted trans-evangelical voice for world missions. His heart belongs to the hurting people who inhabit our globe. *The Missions Addiction* is the expression of God's heart and His invitation to be His partner in giving hope and salvation to the world for whom Christ died.

—T. L. OSBORN
OSFO INTERNATIONAL

David Shibley's diagnosis and *The Missions Addiction* prescription are for every believer. God equips, the Spirit empowers, and His purposes come to pass. Take joy in participating in God's great work by spending each day for eternity . . . for others . . . by becoming a "world Christian." Realize the urgency to bring the Good News to all people and to all nations . . . now!

—MICHAEL D. LITTLE, PRESIDENT
THE CHRISTIAN BROADCASTING NETWORK, INC.

David Shibley is one of the frontline warriors for missions and a man with impeccable integrity and a missions passion. He gives insights out of his own treasures. This book will certainly encourage and equip the leader. I highly recommend it.

—FRANK DAMAZIO, SENIOR PASTOR
PORTLAND CITY BIBLE CHURCH

You have a unique role to play in the literal fulfillment of the Great Commission. *The Missions Addiction* will help you identify what that role is and how God can use you to help give six billion people an opportunity to say yes to Jesus! But let me WARN you: My friend David Shibley incarnates the missions addiction. By reading this book you also may "catch the bug" for world evangelization!

—MIKE DOWNEY, FOUNDER/PRESIDENT
GLOBAL MISSIONS FELLOWSHIP

David Shibley is a most unusual man. He is an informed yet passionate advocate for unreached peoples. Dr. Shibley is a dynamic activist, yet remains a careful, reflective thinker who deeply desires that missional action reflect the whole truth of Scripture. In his most recent book, *The Missions Addiction,* both of these traits, reflection and action, are graphically on display. Your passion for God and His love affair with the nations will challenge you, and your mind will also be illuminated by David Shibley's prophetic biblical message.

—PAUL MCKAUGHAN, PRESIDENT
EVANGELICAL FELLOWSHIP OF MISSION AGENCIES

The Missions Addiction

David Shibley

Charisma®
HOUSE
Books about Spirit-Led Living

THE MISSIONS ADDICTION by David Shibley
Published by Charisma House
A part of Strang Communications Company
600 Rinehart Road
Lake Mary, Florida 32746
www.charismahouse.com

Unless otherwise noted, all Scripture quotations
are from the New King James Version of the Bible.
Copyright ©1979, 1980, 1982 by Thomas Nelson, Inc., publishers.
Used by permission.

Scripture quotations marked AMP are from the Amplified Bible. Old
Testament copyright © 1965, 1987 by the Zondervan Corporation. The
Amplified New Testament copyright © 1954, 1958, 1987 by the
Lockman Foundation. Used by permission.

Scripture quotations marked KJV are from the
King James Version of the Bible.

Scripture quotations marked THE MESSAGE
are from The Message, copyright © 1993, 1994, 1995.
Used by permission of NavPress Publishing Group.

Scripture quotations marked NAS are from the New
American Standard Bible. Copyright ©1960, 1962, 1963, 1968, 1971,
1972, 1973, 1975, 1977 by the Lockman Foundation.
Used by permission. (www.Lockman.org)

Scripture quotations marked NIV are from the Holy
Bible, New International Version. Copyright © 1973, 1978,
1984, International Bible Society. Used by permission.

Scripture quotations marked NLT are from the Holy
Bible, New Living Translation, copyright © 1996.
Used by permission of Tyndale House Publishers, Inc.,
Wheaton, IL 60189. All rights reserved.

Cover design by Michael Bailey Graphic Design

Copyright © 2001 by David Shibley
All rights reserved

Library of Congress Card Number: 2001089666
International Standard Book Number: 0-88419-772-7

01 02 03 04   8 7 6 5 4 3 2 1
Printed in the United States of America

To Naomi

Since 1972, the love of my life,
God's perfect choice for me,
precious companion in life and ministry.

Her worth is far above rubies.
—PROVERBS 31:10

Contents

Foreword

Every Christian must read this book! This book will describe the adventure we are all called to be involved in as Christians. Once again, David Shibley has taken his years of study and statesman perspective to help us all understand in a very simple way what Christians have been struggling to accomplish ever since Jesus commanded us to reach the world. He has made the plight of the world as clear as possible so that a new generation might really understand.

As American Christians, we tend to think that "missionaries are everywhere," but the fact is there are still a lot of places that have never had their first chance to even hear about the gospel. We tend to think that the only people who should be *involved* in missions are people who are *interested* in missions, but the fact is that every Christian has a part in the Great Commission. In fact, the Great Commission is the great adventure of Christianity. Here Dr. Shibley has made the challenge before us so clear that we are left without an excuse.

He unveils what seems to be complicated so that every Christian can know exactly where we stand at this point in history and what it will take to finish the task. The adventure of a lifetime is joining in the adventure of eternity and assisting God Almighty and accomplishing what's on His heart. As you read, you will realize we are right on the edge of the final chapter of completing the task. The question will command your conscience to ask, "What can I do to find my place on the cutting edge?"

You will feel informed, encouraged, inspired and challenged to make your life count for the greatest task in the history of mankind. Once you understand that we are in the completion phase of this task, the only thing left to do is to find your place in it. You will find yourself asking this question: What in the world have Christians been doing for centuries, sitting in churches and going to "Christian" services while so many others have never had a chance? Once you understand the plight of the world, you will be addicted to seeing that same world reached with the gospel of Christ, and it is in that addiction that you find the joy of the Father's heart as you personally take steps each day to help finish the task.

—RON LUCE, PRESIDENT
TEEN MANIA MINISTRIES

My absolute conviction from all the research and gathering of information is that we are in the finishing straight of the marathon for world evangelization.
—PATRICK JOHNSTONE

God has given us a clear and simple task to finish: to see that Christ is worshiped and followed in every people. This is the essential missionary task. This we must do with utmost focus and passion until it is finished.
—RALPH WINTER AND BRUCE KOCH

I know that the gospel is the power of God—the great means that He employs for the regeneration of our ruined world.
—DAVID LIVINGSTONE

ONE

Harvest Hope

For assuredly, I say to you that many prophets and righteous men desired to see what you see, and did not see it, and to hear what you hear, and did not hear it.
—MATTHEW 13:17

And there were loud voices in heaven, saying, "The kingdoms of this world have become the kingdoms of our Lord and of His Christ, and He shall reign forever and ever!"
—REVELATION 11:15

Loud laughter filled the SUV as David Hatley and I bounced to the bumps of the dusty, unpaved back roads in Kenya. The joy in that car was so thick you could almost cut it. We were on our way to one of two orphanages David and his wife, Jennifer, have established. Suddenly David turned to me with a gleam in his eye and said, "This is all your fault!"

"What do you mean?" I asked.

"I was just a happy, Jesus-loving guy who owned a car parts store," he told me. "Then you preached that message that Sunday afternoon in 1983. You called for those who would go with the gospel. Well, now we've raised our family here in

1

Kenya. Africa is our home. We've trained indigenous leaders who oversee eighty-five churches. What a way to live!"

It's too late for David and Jennifer. They will never be "normal" again; a "world Christian serum" has been injected into their spiritual bloodstream. They've been carriers for almost twenty years. They have the missions addiction.

WARNING: IT'S VERY CONTAGIOUS

Like thousands of his young contemporaries, Joel Johnson knew there had to be more to life than parties and popularity. In his pursuit of God, he took a summer missions trip with Teen Mania. That's where he contracted the missions addiction. Today Joel spearheads five outreach teams known as Servants of the Call. They challenge church youth groups across America to be part of a new millennium youth missions movement. They are seeing God's Spirit move powerfully in scores of churches. Not satisfied with being missions addicts themselves, they are out to hook a whole generation!

John, Troy and Terry Henry head two companies in Texas. These young brothers are creative, energetic and entrepreneurial. Their companies are thriving. Their passion, however, is not to build companies but to build the kingdom of God. Through times of economic blessings and challenges, they give strategically and generously to advance the gospel. It's because of their missions addiction.

Yvonne Wood is a very capable young woman with a master of divinity degree. After taking the Perspectives on the World Christian Movement course, she became missions addicted. Now she coordinates the Nashville branch of the U.S. Center for World Mission and has become a catalyst for uniting area churches for evangelistic outreaches and joint missions projects.

David Thomas, an Oklahoma pastor, had not ministered

overseas until I invited him to be part of the teaching team at Global Advance's Frontline Shepherds Conference in Kisumu, Kenya. On that trip God broke his heart for pastoral leaders in developing nations. Now David has given his entire life to helping equip pastors in needy countries who have few opportunities for training. He caught the missions addiction.

Dick and Suzie Bashta are joyfully obsessed with the hope of seeing God worshiped in every culture and by all peoples on earth. Through an amazing unfolding of events, Dick is now president of Adopt-a-People Clearinghouse.[1] They work with The Bible League to help ensure both culturally relevant churches and Scripture in the vernacular of literally "every tribe, people and nation." The Bashtas have a chronic case of missions addiction.

Peter and Heather Armstrong are a young married couple who recently graduated from John Brown University in Arkansas. As part of an advertising class project, they realized there was no comprehensive list to help match those interested in short-term missions outreaches with corresponding opportunities. Today, just a year later, hundreds of missions agencies post their opportunities on the website the Armstrongs helped create—www.shorttermmissions.com. On a shoestring budget, with tremendous opposition in spiritual warfare, they persevered as part of a new breed of technology-savvy missions addicts. Now an entirely new entity exists for cooperative efforts.

This addiction is private as well as public. Some one hundred ninety million missions addicts quietly hide away with God every day and intercede for the evangelization of the world. These "closet world changers" have an incessant craving—they crave God's glory among all peoples. Their only temporary "high" is when they themselves worship God, knowing that their worship is a little foretaste of the global glory to God their prayers are helping bring into reality.

These folks are hooked. But as David Hatley said, "What a way to live!"

A MISSIONS ADDICTION?

The Bible tells how Stephanas and his family had "addicted themselves to the ministry of the saints" (1 Cor. 16:15, KJV). The Greek verb *tasso*, translated in the King James Version as "addicted," carries the idea of being *set* or *appointed*. Several translations say that Stephanas and his family "devoted themselves" to this ministry. Further study of the original word shows that it means "to place or station in a fixed spot."[2] It can also mean "to order, determine or appoint," which is how Luke uses the word in Acts 18:2, describing how Claudius, the Roman proconsul, had "ordered" all Jews to leave Rome (NIV). The verb is used in Acts 28:23 to recount how Paul was given an "appointed" day to make his case for the gospel to the Jewish leaders at Rome.

Drawing from this biblical use of the word, *a missions addiction* is a willful fixation on God's purpose in history—the enthroning of Jesus Christ in every culture and people. It is a voluntary, *magnificent obsession.* Those with the missions addiction have their faith and focus on what is final—the Father's hot resolve that Jesus will reign over all the earth and receive worship from every tribe, people and nation. If you have contracted the missions addiction, you are *set* heart and soul on Christ and His global honor. You are *stationed in a fixed spot,* as a soldier on duty, faithful at your post but poised for new assignments. You feel a divine sense of destiny that you have been *appointed* by God to extend His glory. Indeed, Jesus has *ordered* you to go to every people and turn His enemies into loyal worshipers (Matt. 28:19).

Notice the clear differences between the missions addiction and unrighteous addictions: The missions addiction is a *willful* addiction, one which we enter with eyes wide open. We are not duped—or doped—by this addiction. We fully understand the consequences of this fixation with God's global glory. In contrast to the tragedy of drug or alcohol addicts who are dulled from reality, this addiction makes everything in us snap to attention! We are suddenly sensitized to the flow of events as they relate to God's grander scheme. Unrighteous addictions distract people and render them unable to cope. The missions addiction brings laser focus and empowers us as transformation agents for individuals, whole cultures, even entire nations.

Another biblical Greek word aptly describes our times. It is the word *kairos,* a word Scripture reserves for unique seasons of possibilities. By sovereign grace God has chosen that your life be woven into this *kairos* hour for world evangelization. Almost always in the Bible, *kairos* refers to a brief, exponentially heightened season of God's favor. Using this word, Jesus spoke of a "time of harvest" in Matthew 13:30, and Paul spoke of a "due season" for reaping in Galatians 6:9. In such *kairos* seasons of opportunity the Bible urges us to be "redeeming the time" (Eph. 5:16). One translation reads, "Buying up each opportunity" (AMP).

The breakup of the old Soviet Union and the opening of the Eastern bloc to the gospel over a decade ago was something of a trial balloon the Holy Spirit was sending up. He was asking us, "What will you do with mega-opportunities? Will you be a righteous steward of this *kairos* season? Are you *stationed* to leverage this hour of opportunity? Will you finally seize your destiny and align your life's purpose with the purposes of God in your generation? *Are you ready for the missions addiction?*"

When our sons were small, my wife, Naomi, and I would tuck our boys into their beds at night and sing to them. But it was no lullaby! As they drifted off to sleep, we would sing:

Rise up, O men of God,
Have done with lesser things.
Give heart and soul and mind and strength
To serve the King of kings![3]

Let me ask you point blank: Is your heart still wrapped around "lesser things"? When is it going to end? When will *your* priorities line up with *God's* priorities? *When?*

The missions addiction is first and foremost a passion for Jesus. Flowing from our love for Him, we are passionate to see all peoples love and worship Him, too. We dare not reverse the order and become more enamored with the missions cause than with Christ Himself. Whenever ministry *for* Christ overtakes relationship *with* Him, we are headed for spiritual disaster. But out of the enrichment of a growing love relationship with Him, we are compelled by the love of Christ into missions.[4] As a missionary to Muslims, Henry Martyn said, "The Spirit of Christ is the spirit of missions, and the nearer we get to Him, the more intensely missionary we become."

Francis Xavier stood on an island looking toward what seemed to him to be the rock-hard resistance of China's millions. As this missionary looked toward China's mainland he cried, "Rock, rock, when will you open to my Savior?" Xavier sent word back to Europe urging the dispassionate students of his day to be missions addicted. He pled with them, saying, "Tell the students to give up their small ambitions and come eastward to preach the gospel of Christ!"

What are you giving your life for? And why?

DAVID LIVINGSTONE, GENOMES AND E-VANGELISM

There are those reading these words who are churning on the inside even as you read. Something deep inside knows that, like Esther, "you have come to the kingdom for such a time as this" (Esther 4:14). And what a time it is!

Someone has observed that history now comes equipped with a fast forward button. Today we no longer speak of needing a change of pace. Rather, we are caught in the tidal wave of the pace of change. The cloning of Dolly in 1997 launched humanity into a brave new eugenics world of selective breeding. The decoding of the genetic message began in 1990 and is now substantially complete. We now know the genome's sequence of 3.2 billion DNA units.[5] This opens the door to hopeful possibilities for personalized remedies, but it may also be a Pandora's box of horrors. Dolly may prove to be a "wolf in sheep's clothing."

Many sociologists believe we are currently in a third industrial revolution. The first, the Industrial Era, gave machines massive strength. The second revolution, the Information Era, also gave these machines hyperintelligence and even senses. The third and current revolution, the Bionomic Era, is the merging of brain and biology. DNA (which stores information) and microchips (which process information) are now being combined, with the flow of information going from one to the other.

Speaking of information, the Internet has literally put the world at our fingertips. Millions search for truth amidst its unending data. Thankfully, many *are* finding the truth as innovative forms of *e-vangelism* present the gospel to cyberseekers. The Internet is a boon for the church and for the flow of missions information. It is also a tool that pulls millions into deception and bondage. Therefore, we should be flooding this information highway with the gospel—pure and simple. Let's take a lesson from history and not fall prey to the error of separatist fundamentalists who disdained earlier technologies as "of the devil" because of their evil potential. Rather, as God's Word admonishes, "Do not be overcome by evil, but overcome evil with good" (Rom. 12:21).

Into this sometimes frightening world—a world with no road maps from previous travelers to help us—Jesus calls us to bear His name, extend His glory and fulfill His commission. Missions cannot and should not live in a "David Livingstone paradigm" that sees the task through nineteenth-century lenses. Many enemies, and even a few friends, still perceive missions as a sort of Victorian-era anachronism. Yet it has been my experience that the freshest, most innovative thinkers in the body of Christ today are people with the missions addiction. Far from living in the past, most missions strategists are thinking decades into the future.

Norman Barnes, a missions specialist living in England, believes that the rapidity of change and our ability to adapt and accommodate global change are key issues for world missions. "The electronic world has made and will continue to make major changes in evangelism, but the gospel is still incarnational," he observes. "We still need church planters to go to unreached areas and peoples, but globalization and the technology revolution have opened wider opportunities to a greater number of people to be involved in the harvest."[6]

Charles Fishman writes, "Creating change, managing it, mastering it and surviving it is the agenda for anyone in business who aims to make a difference."[7] It is true in missions as well. Note that phrase—"creating change." We are not merely to adapt well to enforced change, but we are to be intentional agents of change ourselves. And there is plenty that needs changing, as we will see in the next chapter.

Jesus predicted a time when the wheat and tares would grow up together—a time of both deception and true harvest.[8] He also said that the missions mandate would accelerate in the milieu of global ecological disasters, man-made catastrophes and false messiahs. In other words, Jesus was talking about our day. He said these "sorrows" were actually "birth pangs," pushing humanity into His New World Order. Running parallel to these events, "this gospel of the kingdom will be preached in all the world as a witness to all the nations, and then the end will come" (Matt. 24:14).

Amidst this hyperchange, just as Jesus prophesied, world evangelization is racing at record speed. "Our eternal God . . . is proactive, dynamic, moving by His Holy Spirit in unprecedented ways," writes missions expert Grant McClung. "In the exciting mix of theology and technology, followers of Christ are challenged to keep the first-century reality connected to the twenty-first-century context." He continues, "Don't be left behind in this final global 'spiritual revolution.' Bring every energy and focus to 'click on' to be online with what the God of history/God of the nations is doing in your world. In connecting to God's work in your world, you—and those you bring with you—will be on your way toward becoming a 'globalbeliever.com' with world Christian values and ministries."[9]

Clearly, God is accelerating His global activity. "For He will finish the work and cut it short in righteousness, because the LORD will make a short work upon the earth" (Rom. 9:28). Paul quotes Isaiah to remind us of God's rapid judgment at the end of the age. But there is also a quick, almost "instantly ripe" harvest God is producing before our eyes as more people are responding to the gospel than ever in history. How will all this affect evangelism, missions and church life in the next few years? No one is quite sure just yet.

Those who are not lucid and pliable in the hands of the Holy Spirit will experience both the alienation of hyperchange and the gut-level knowing that they are out of sync with the "new thing" God is unfolding. That is why inverted churches with placid global vision look more like twentieth-century dinosaurs with each passing week.

Just reading the last few paragraphs may be exhausting. How can we hope for spiritual and emotional equilibrium in this out-of-kilter "Brave New World"? We must become more intimate than ever with the God who is orchestrating history. Jim Reapsome reminds us, "Perhaps we have too often assumed that good missionaries can ride with the punches. Most of all, we need spiritual reinforcement for our souls. The titans of missionary service are those who know God so intimately that regardless of changes, they do not surrender. They are like the wise man who built his house on the rock—and that rock is Jesus."[10]

There is a rock where our hopes can anchor. There are some things that never change. They escape the traumas of transition because they transcend fashion or prevailing sentiments. In fact, these verities transcend time itself.

A FIRM FOUNDATION

Sometimes the earth itself seems to be realigning underneath us. But there is still a firm foundation for the faithful. First and foremost, *the character of God has not changed*. He has not changed—He *cannot* change. "I am the LORD," He declares, "I do not change" (Mal. 3:6).

The Scriptures have not changed. A. W. Tozer was right: "The Word of God is the antibiotic that seeks out and destroys the viruses that would plague the life of the church."[11] God's Word is eternal: "The grass withers, the flower fades, but the word of our God stands forever" (Isa. 40:8).

The gospel has not changed. Methods to communicate the gospel are in constant flux, but the gospel itself never changes. Yet some religious leaders today are trumpeting an uncertain sound about the very nature of salvation. To say the least, it can be a confusing time theologically. But for Christians who hold Scripture as the paramount authority, there is no uncertainty and no confusion. A recent important document, "The Gospel of Jesus Christ: An Evangelical Celebration," says it well:

We affirm that Jesus Christ is the only way of salvation, the only mediator between God and humanity (John 14:6; 1 Tim. 2:5). We deny that anyone is saved in any other way than by

Jesus Christ and His Gospel. The Bible offers
no hope that sincere worshipers of other
religions will be saved without personal faith
in Jesus Christ.[12]

There can be no firmer foundation than Jesus Christ and
His saving power. It is an anchor that will hold when everything else shakes off its hinges. I have experienced the
redemptive lift of the gospel personally and in my family's
heritage. I have also seen the gospel's transforming power
around the world.

A few years ago after I had preached in a church in India,
a woman with a big smile came to me with tears in her eyes.
"I've been hoping for ten years that you would come back to
this city," she began. "I've always wanted to thank you personally. Do you remember when you preached an evangelistic crusade in this city a decade ago?"

"Yes," I said, "I'll always remember that crusade."

"Well, my husband attended just one night of that gospel
meeting," she continued. "He had never heard the gospel
before. From his childhood he had worshiped idols. But
when you preached Christ that night and challenged the lis-
teners to commit their lives to Christ, my husband publicly
responded." By this time we were both crying.

"That night after the meeting, my husband came home
and quietly walked through our house, gathering every relic
and idol. He put them in a big pile outside our house and
burned them all to ashes. Then he called me and our children together and announced, 'As of tonight there is a new
Lord over our family, and His name is Jesus Christ!'

"I just wanted to say thank you," she told me again. "Our
family was forever changed from that one night and that one
hearing of the gospel."

That is the transforming power of the gospel. No wonder
Paul said, "For I am not ashamed of the gospel of Christ, for

it is the power of God to salvation for everyone who believes, for the Jew first and also for the Greek" (Rom. 1:16).

Finally, *the Great Commission has not changed*—nor has it been rescinded. Amy Carmichael often referred to the missions mandate as "the great unrepealed commission." Ever since Jesus issued that commission, the church's purpose has been pristine and clear. *The purpose of the church is to bring God glory through the worldwide proclamation, reception and worship of His Son.* This is our corporate purpose. It should be our individual purpose as well. As D. L. Moody said, "Never think that Jesus commanded a trifle, nor dare to trifle with anything He has commanded."

This is a book about God's passion for the world. God's bottom-line passion for the world is not just to save people from perdition—although this is a wonderful, essential part of the Good News. God's core passion is to see *every* tribe and people passionately worship Him. The true mission of God in the earth is not only a rescue operation—it is a loving Father searching for a bride for His Son. As Paul Billheimer observed, "Romance is at the heart of the universe." In the marital union, the bride typically assumes the surname of the groom. That is exactly what happened as "God . . . visited the Gentiles to take out of them a people for His name" (Acts 15:14).

The *Westminster Shorter Catechism* asks, "What is the sole purpose of man?" The answer is simple, profound and biblical: "The sole purpose of man is to glorify God and to enjoy Him forever." How, then, do we glorify God? We glorify Him by obedience to His directives, drawing on the power of His life in us. In other words, the most God-honoring, purpose-satisfying, destiny-fulfilling life is a life controlled by the Holy Spirit and fully submissive to His promptings and clear commands.

When you have the missions addiction, suddenly denominational affiliations and even less-structured networks hold little interest for you. In heart, your new "community of faith" includes "world Christians" across the gamut of the body of Christ, those who, like you, are passionate for God's glory among the nations. Your creed is simple and clear. You align with God-chasers all over the world who race with His life and light to the ends of the earth. C. Peter Wagner describes these world Christians as those who "share an honest mutual desire to obey the Scriptures, serve our Lord, receive the maximum fullness of the Holy Spirit and get on with the task of winning our world to Christ. As a result, Christians around the world are more united in heart, mind and spirit than they possibly have been for centuries."[13]

Few would question that we're in a late hour in God's prophetic timetable. It's too late to be little, too near the end to be frivolous. I like Leonard Ravenhill's answer when he was asked, "Do you believe we're living in the last days?" "I believe we're living in *your* last days," Ravenhill responded.

This is not only our *best* shot at the global harvest, but it's also our *only* shot. When it comes to your target and the direction of your life's influence, aim well.

STATE OF THE WORLD

Suppose a glass is set in front of you, and there is water in the glass halfway to the top. Is the glass half empty, or is it half full? It depends on your perspective.

It's the same when we begin to report God's work around the world. Some statistics indicate we are losing the battle for world evangelization. Other measurements suggest convincingly that we are advancing toward the goal of "a church for every people and the gospel for every person."[14] I am personally convinced that there were dramatic advances for the gospel worldwide in the 1990s and that those previous ten years were a mere prelude to what God will do in this decade.

However, we should not oversimplify the task. The toughest

unreached peoples remain unreached for that very reason—penetrating those peoples and cultures with the light of the gospel is the most daunting challenge we have ever faced in missions. David Hesselgrave has observed, "If the futurologists I have read are correct, twenty-first-century missionaries will inherit a challenging and even chaotic world. But natural disasters, social upheaval, moral decline and religious confusion entail opportunities to demonstrate concern, togetherness, holiness and commitment. The new century . . . will certainly present tremendous opportunities to demonstrate the truth and power of Christ."[15]

There seems to be considerable debate regarding the world's fastest-growing faith—is it Christianity or Islam? In some ways, Islam is growing faster than Christianity, if one includes all expressions of Christianity in the figures. Using this standard, Islam's growth rate of 2.15 percent annually exceeds Christianity's rate of 1.45 percent. However, it's important to note that 96 percent of Islam's growth is biological growth, children born to Muslims. But conversion growth is quite another matter. According to figures in the 2000 edition of the *World Christian Encyclopedia,* some 950,000 people convert to Islam annually from another religion. Christianity, however, sees some 2.7 million converts each year from another religious persuasion.[16] In fact, in the last decade, the number of born-again Christians in the world doubled! Of a total world population of over six billion, roughly 33 percent identify themselves as Christian. Evangelical or Bible-believing Christians today number 647 million, or 11 percent of the world's population. In other words, one in every eight people in the world is a Bible-believing Christian. As Patrick Johnstone observes, "Evangelical Christians are the fastest-growing major religious group in the world today, and it is the only one growing rapidly by conversion."[17]

I believe God is going to exceptional lengths to bring His light and love to the Islamic world. Dr. Dudley Woodbury, an eminent authority on ministry to Muslims, says his students have documented over six hundred conversions of former Muslims where dreams and visions were prominent.[18] It seems clear that there are numerous Christophanies—literal appearances of Christ—to Muslims around the world.

Further, as Paul reminds us, "God has not cast away His people whom He foreknew" (Rom. 11:2). God is using current events to highlight His love for the Jewish people and point them to Yeshua. Robert Stearns reports, "Politically, for the last several years an 'antimissionary' bill has been introduced to the Knesset [the legislature in Israel] that calls for even more curtailing of religious freedom. However, as God has promised, this has only served to work for the good of the Messianic community . . . Through the publicity surrounding this bill and the international opposition it has received, they have discovered that it is not just a few isolated Jews who believe in Yeshua, but several thousand in the land and tens of thousands around the world."[19]

Major milestones toward world evangelism have been reached. Every Home for Christ workers have systematically distributed gospel booklets to over two billion households in two hundred nations with over twenty-six million recorded responses. And as of January 1, 2001, the *JESUS* film had been seen by over four billion people, with 128,873,719 people registering decisions for Christ![20] This has to be the most staggering evangelistic triumph in the church's history—and you have lived to see it!

Equally thrilling is the amazing progress in penetrating unreached peoples with the gospel. The Joshua Project of the AD 2000 and Beyond Movement reports that the number of people groups without a church of at least one hundred members or an active church-planting movement continues to shrink. The AD 2000's original Joshua Project list stood at 1,739 in the mid-1990s. Recently adjusted, the number stands at 1,510. As of 1999, only 195 of the groups on the

Joshua Project list had yet to be targeted or claimed, according to Doug Lucas of *Brigada Today*.[21] In the 10/40 Window—the geographic region of the world with the most unreached peoples—amazing progress occurred in a recent two-year period. In March 1998, of the 1,510 targeted people groups of the Joshua Project 2000, fifty of those groups had a church of one hundred or more believers in a reproducing fellowship. By April 2000, 476 of the targeted groups had a church of one hundred or more believers![22] Recent emphasis on the "40/70 Window"—including the Balkans, Russia and Turkey—indicates that God will continue to be at work dramatically in the most gospel-needy (and gospel-responsive) areas of the world in this decade. This includes both the 10/40 Window and the 40/70 Window.

But there are sobering statistics as well that remind us that the task is far from finished. Dr. David Barrett says that the percentage of Christians in the world has remained substantially unchanged at 33 percent. He projects that percentage to stay flat for the next quarter century. Barrett also believes that some four thousand groups (substantially more than other lists) have no viable Christian witness.[23]

According to missions statistician Justin Long, there was a net increase of about nine million people in 2000 in the unevangelized world. Also in A.D. 2000, more than eighty million unevangelized heard the gospel, and more than nineteen million put their faith in Christ. Of those who rejected Him, twenty-one million died as evangelized non-Christians. This year 13.2 million died never once hearing the good news of Christ.[24]

There is much left to do. And that is the reason why God has sovereignly allowed you to pick up this book. He wants you as an "eleventh-hour worker" in His harvest.

Paul Eshelman, director of the *JESUS* film project for Campus Crusade for Christ, reminds us that this whole issue isn't ultimately about numbers—it's about Jesus and people who need Him. Eshelman urges us to press on to every people, every person: "We had named 2000 as the year by which we wanted to get the Gospel to every person in the world. In one sense, we have made staggering strides toward that goal beyond anything we've ever seen before. In another sense, we haven't completed the task yet, so we'll keep going. Our purpose in life is not to complete goals. Our purpose in life is to reconcile people who don't know God back to Him. That's what He's called us to do for the rest of our lives."[25]

Concerning the harvest, Jesus was both an optimist ("the harvest is plentiful") and a realist ("the laborers are few"). We should minister from that framework—no hype and no despair. Jesus will write the final chapter; it is *His* harvest.

NOT YOUR FATHER'S MISSIONS PROGRAM

This premiere decade of the twenty-first century finds the church in a position to receive both greater harvest and greater hostility than ever in history. What is on the horizon for the next few years? The following predictions are not prophecies, although many of these observations are based on biblical promises or clear spiritual trends. These predictions are by no means infallible. They are based on what I've seen in ministry in fifty-one nations and what I sense deep in my spirit. I believe we can expect to see some, if not all, of the following scenarios.

1. IN THE PROVIDENCE OF GOD, THIS WILL BE A DECADE OF CONTINUED COLOSSAL SPIRITUAL HARVEST.

The seeds of harvest planted by the massive prayer movements of the nineties will bear great fruit in this decade. The church should press in for no less than one billion souls worldwide in this decade. However, we must remember that this harvest will not reap itself. Large numbers of anointed laborers must be dispatched to the ripened fields—and fast.

2. THERE WILL BE INCREASED CONFLICT FOR THE CHURCH.

Christians are perceived by many as "the new bigots" because of what unbelievers view as a "narrow and prejudicial" insistence that Jesus is the only way of salvation. Presently, the American church is ill prepared for intensified criticism and persecution, and this may cause a significant reduction in some church memberships and attendance.

3. RELIGIONS WILL BECOME MORE MILITANT, ESPECIALLY ISLAM.

Radicals in historically tolerant religions like Buddhism and Hinduism will intensify their attacks on Christians as greater numbers from their ranks profess faith in Jesus. Already, evangelistic inroads among ancient religions are perceived as threatening. As we impact more—and eventually all—of the remaining unreached peoples, the numbers of Christian martyrs may rise dramatically. We must be more militant against demonic opposition and at the same time become increasingly gracious and winsome among non-Christians.

4. BUSINESS AND MEDIA MEGA-THINKERS WILL EMERGE WHO WILL HELP THE TWENTY-FIRST-CENTURY CHURCH THINK OUTSIDE THE BOX.

These new entrepreneurs will break new ground in evangelism and missions. "Techno-Spurgeons" will express eloquence through powerful visual communication. These twenty-first-century communicators are not preachers, but producers of highly innovative media presentations of the gospel. They will either replace or complement those with well-honed pulpit skills.

5. THERE WILL BE A MORE EXACTING STANDARD FOR CHRISTIAN LEADERSHIP.

The pretentiousness of some major Christian leaders, especially in the United States and Africa, will not be allowed in this decade either by God or by the people to whom they minister.

6. THE CHARISMATIC WING OF THE CHURCH IN AMERICA WILL IDENTIFY MORE DISTINCTLY WITH THE POOR AND DOWNTRODDEN.

They will become a stronger prophetic voice on behalf of those who have no voice—aborted children, the abused, the diseased and the dispossessed. This will win both new friends and vicious enemies and will ameliorate the abuses of some extreme prosperity teaching of the 1980s and 1990s.

7. THE EARLY YEARS OF THIS CENTURY WILL SEE MASSIVE TRANSITION AS GOD POSTURES A NEW GENERATION FOR LEADERSHIP.

Young missions visionaries will be mentored by those who will be called Joshuas and Calebs—seasoned veterans who are able to transcend eras and help direct younger visionaries. Jesus Movement II will continue to spread. Just as there was a global MTV generation in the 1990s, there will be a young global Jesus generation in this decade.

8. THE MIRACULOUS WILL BE INCREASINGLY COMMONPLACE, AND THE LINES BETWEEN TRADITIONAL EVANGELICALS AND CHARISMATICS WILL CONTINUE TO BLUR.

By the end of the decade it may be a moot issue, with the overwhelming majority of Bible-believing Christians endorsing and experiencing present-day signs and wonders. The church will live in Hebrews 11: Some heroes of the faith will experience miraculous interventions while others will be martyred. Either way, they are *all* heroes of the faith.

9. WE WILL ALSO LIVE IN MATTHEW 24, WITH ACCELERATED NATURAL DISASTERS, ETHNIC-BASED CONFLICTS AND RELIGIOUS DECEPTION. AT THE SAME TIME THE GOSPEL WILL PROGRESS WITH RECORD SPEED.

Rogue nations and terrorist groups may attempt nuclear blackmail. This level of natural and man-made distress will cause many to turn to God. Others will harden their hearts, wondering "how a loving God could allow these things to happen."

10. MAJOR JEWISH AND MUSLIM LEADERS WILL PUBLICLY DECLARE THEIR FAITH IN JESUS AS THEIR LORD.

Some will be killed as a result. Realizing the threat, these leaders will place their testimony on video, which will receive wide Internet and underground distribution.

11. EVANGELICAL THEOLOGY AND EXPERIENTIAL WORSHIP WILL BLEND INTO A FRESH, POWERFUL EXPRESSION OF NEW MILLENNIUM CHRISTIANITY.

Pentecostals and charismatics who once derided the need for apologetics will embrace it because of embarrassing and blatantly unbiblical teaching by a few of their highest-profile preachers. Also, the influences of postmodernism within the church will heighten the need for biblical understanding. Conversely, many evangelicals will sense a dearth in their own spirituality and move either toward a mystic form of Orthodoxy or charismatic worship.

12. THE GLOBAL CHURCH WILL BE MORE INTERCONNECTED THAN EVER.

The under-40s in the Western church will be alive with missions passion. Many of them will date their missions addiction back to the short-term missions trips they took as students in the nineties. Massive churches will continue to be spawned in Latin America and Asia. A biblical "remnant" church will begin to turn back the plague of AIDS in Africa as discipleship impacts the continent as forcibly in this decade as evangelistic crusades did in the 1980s and 1990s.

No doubt God has many other surprises for us. For instance, Jack Hayford sees these possibilities in the next couple of decades:

. . . lines between Christians formerly
segmented as evangelicals, Pentecostals,
charismatics, fundamentalists, Reformed, Bible
Church and so on have vaporized. Persecution
birthed a prayer-begotten unity; plus the Holy

Spirit outpouring upon youth (the "Hyper-Jesus" awakening of 2003–2007) precipitated this uniting force. It was the vigor, passion and honesty of these young people that faced the church with a crisis: The new generation of young leaders refused to sustain past separatism in the body of Christ. Still, with humility, they embraced the wisdom of pastors and leaders who focused "The Way"—essential biblical truths for proclamation and discipleship.[26]

What an incredible time to identify with Christ and to carry the missions addiction! We have lived to see at least the early stages of the shaking prophesied in Scripture:

The phrase "one last shaking" means a thorough housecleaning, getting rid of all the historical and religious junk so that the unshakable essentials stand clear and uncluttered. Do you see what we've got? An unshakable kingdom! And do you see how thankful we must be? Not only thankful, but brimming with worship, deeply reverent before God. For God is not an indifferent bystander. He's actively cleaning house, torching all that needs to burn, and he won't quit until it's all cleansed. God himself is Fire!
—Hebrews 12:27–29, The Message

UNSHAKABLE KINGDOM, UNSTOPPABLE CHURCH

What has brought us to this awesome hour is a *great covenant* (Gen. 12:1–3) and a *Great Commission* (Matt. 28:19; Mark 16:15). God swore to Abraham that his seed would bless all

the families of the earth. Jesus reiterated this covenant commission when He ordered us to turn all these families into
His friends through the gospel. We are hopeful because of a
great completion God promised Abraham and incessantly reaffirms throughout Scripture. Indeed, in the last book of the
Bible, John prophetically sees God's promise to Abraham
made good—redeemed men and women from every people
worshiping God and His sacrificial Lamb for the extravagant
mercies bestowed on them.

**After these things I looked, and behold, a great
multitude which no one could number, of all
nations, tribes, peoples, and tongues, standing
before the throne and before the Lamb,
clothed with white robes, with palm branches
in their hands, and crying out with a loud
voice, saying, "Salvation belongs to our God
who sits on the throne, and to the Lamb!"**
—REVELATION 7:9–10

This great covenant, commission and completion impel us
to a *great commitment* to be God's instruments for mission—
accomplished. We have entered the season Amos saw in the
spirit when "the plowman shall overtake the reaper" (Amos
9:13). He saw a time of such colossal ingathering that harvest
would literally pile on top of harvest! It is that prophetic season of hyperharvest where God has positioned your life!
Twenty centuries of believers are cheering us on from heaven's
arena (Heb. 12:1). Globalization has opened the door for history's greatest harvest, but there is an Achilles heel that could
keep us from seeing this harvest hope realized.

What could stop us? Hear Pastor Ted Haggard's assessment:

**I think our greatest enemy is simply *distraction*.
False eschatology, materialism, immorality and
sensuality are begging for our attention. They**

constantly attempt to mire us in muddy
distractions, while the primary purpose of
Christ's Great Commission goes unfulfilled.

But if we stay focused and intentional, we
will succeed in every location we target with
prayer and outreach. Governments have been
unable to stop us; resistant religions are
becoming nervous and archaic. Paralyzing the-
ologies are being discredited.

Simply put, if we'll work together and
remain focused on the lost, we will have a generation of explosive growth unlike what we've
seen for 2,000 years. God has set us up for
service to the world.[27]

When it has all been said and done, the worship of Jesus
by every tribe and nation is a "done deal." It was this assurance of Christ's ultimate triumph that sustained William
Carey, the father of modern missions, in his darkest days of
discouragement.

When I left England, my hope of India's
conversion was very strong; but amongst so
many obstacles, it would die, unless upheld by
God. Well, I have God, and His Word is true.
Though the superstitions of the heathen were a
thousand times stronger than they are, and the
example of the Europeans a thousand times
worse; though I were deserted by all and persecuted by all, yet my faith, fixed on the sure
Word, would rise above all obstructions and
overcome every trial. God's cause will triumph.[28]

Perhaps, like Carey, you have been discouraged because of
past failures in evangelism. You have thrown out the net, but
the "catch" has been negligible. You may feel a little like

Peter. Jesus had just challenged him to "launch out into the deep and let down your nets for a catch" (Luke 5:4). Burned out and discouraged, Peter replied, "Master, we have toiled all night and caught nothing" (v. 5).

Is that how you feel? Like Peter, you may say, "I've fought the darkness and toiled through the night. But I have little to show for my efforts."

But Peter didn't factor two new components into the equation that would change everything:

- ■ The night was almost over and the day was breaking!

- ■ Jesus had shown up!

Our Lord is calling on us one more time to cast a wide . . . *wide* . . . net! Don't despair that your previous work has produced little. The night is about to give way to dawn, and Jesus is now on the scene! Like Peter, say to Him, "Nevertheless at Your word I will let down the net" (v. 5). Then get ready for the catch of a lifetime.

The last word of the Greek text of Acts is *unhindered (akolutos)*, an adverb used to describe the unstoppable progress of the gospel from Jerusalem to Rome. The gospel remains unstoppable today. In two thousand years no enemy has been able to forge chains strong enough to halt its incessant advance. This seed of Abraham—this root of Jesse—will ultimately break through the most resistant soil and turn it into fertile ground for His kingdom.

Romans 15 is one of the Bible's great missions chapters. Paul covers the gamut of biblical prophecies to underscore the bedrock assurance that the Messiah will ultimately reign over every people. Then, after applying the weight of God's sworn promises to exalt His Son among every nation, Paul gives one of the Bible's most beautiful benedictions, urging his readers to refresh their souls in the sure hope of Christ's enthronement among all peoples. Let your heart breathe in fresh hope today. Jesus shall reign—and He wants to use you to help make it happen!

"There shall be a root of Jesse; and He who shall rise to reign over the Gentiles, in Him the Gentiles shall hope." Now may the God of hope fill you will all joy and peace in believing, that you may abound in hope by the power of the Holy Spirit.

—ROMANS 15:12-13

One of the fundamental reasons for the failure of the church to implement the Last Command of the Lord Jesus Christ is the lack of the right structures.
—Patrick Johnstone

The most critical issue for missions in the twenty-first century is theological. Are those who have never heard of Christ's saving grace certainly lost? If there is any question about this, the heroic sacrifices of missionaries in the nineteenth and twentieth centuries will not be forthcoming in the twenty-first.
—Robertson McQuilkin

If my faith is false, I ought to change it; whereas, if it be true, I am bound to propagate it.
—Bishop Whatley

TWO

Disaster Prevention

There is salvation in no one else! There is no other name in all of heaven for people to call on to save them.
—ACTS 4:12, NLT

But everything exposed by the light becomes visible, for it is light that makes everything visible. This is why it is said: "Wake up, O sleeper, rise from the dead, and Christ will shine on you." Be very careful, then, how you live—not as unwise but as wise, making the most of every opportunity, because the days are evil. Therefore do not be foolish, but understand what the Lord's will is. Do not get drunk on wine, which leads to debauchery. Instead, be filled with the Spirit.
—EPHESIANS 5:13–18, NIV

I'll never forget the night a demonized man pulled a knife on me in Yuraslov, Russia.

We were in the hotel restaurant after a session for training young leaders. I was sitting with a group of pastors when out of nowhere an intoxicated man made a beeline for me from across the room. He began yelling at me in Russian: "I hate your Jesus! I don't want you here! I'm going to kill you!"

The man literally had me in a corner. There were no hotel security personnel; they had decided to go home earlier that evening since it was a "slow" night. Someone ran and called

27

the police. Instead of the local police responding–the Russian army came! A regiment of the army, recently returned from conflict in Chechnya, was stationed just a few blocks from the hotel. Quickly, three soldiers in battle fatigues burst into the restaurant and took the man and his knife away.

Later we found out that this man had no criminal record and no connection to the Russian Mafia. I'm convinced he was just a man "on assignment" from the devil. The man was not my enemy; he himself was a victim of the enemy. The devil and evil spirits aligned with him are the real enemy. Because we are committed to the praise of Jesus among all nations, Satan has us in his cross hairs.

My heart was still beating fast as one of the Russian soldiers escorted me safely to my room. As I lay on the bed processing what had just happened, I couldn't help but laugh. What a headline that would be: "American Preacher Rescued by Russian Soldiers!"

This is but one of the amazing twists of history God has engineered over the last decade.

He has given our generation the incredible honor of setting the standard and the pace for the honor of His name in this new century and millennium. We have been positioned in an era of remarkable change. God did not make a mistake when He chose you to bear Christ's name at this hinge of history. He knew exactly whom He wanted to carry the light of the gospel in the twenty-first century. He wanted *you*.

As we begin this new millennium, He has intersected your life with a season of spectacular, even unparalleled, opportunity. This period of time is not unlike that which God described to His prophet Habakkuk: "Look among the nations and watch–be utterly astounded! For I will work a work in your days which you would not believe though it were told you" (Hab. 1:5).

Much like a high-speed train, the gospel is proceeding at record speed. More people are coming to Christ than ever in history. Yet the devil would love to "derail" the whole missions enterprise. In this chapter we will look at several potential "train wrecks" that will occur if we get "on the wrong tracks." We will also see how these disasters can be avoided.

> **He has given our generation the incredible honor of setting the standard and the pace for the honor of His name in this new century and millennium.**

In the midst of this unequaled global harvest, many Christians cannot put in the sickle and reap because they are in a dense spiritual fog. They are drowning in trivia and choking on minutia. This brings us to the first potential derailment. We are in grave danger of exporting a legacy of lethargy to the next generation.

A LEGACY OF LETHARGY

I have had the honor of equipping church leaders in over fifty nations. The beauty of the body of Christ expressed through multiple cultures is indescribable. I have drunk deeply from the refreshing wells of the church's life in many nations. So it is more than a little disturbing to discover that American Christians are by far the most self-absorbed believers in the entire world. We whine, "I just want to know my purpose; I've got to reach my destiny." We race all over the country to attend "destiny conferences," and we devour tapes and books on "reaching your full potential." It would be amusing if it were not so appalling. Even cloaking our self-centeredness in Christian garb and jargon cannot cover the nakedness of this cult of self that has infested much of the American church.

How can we ever hope to discover *our* purpose in the earth with little or no interest in *His* purpose? How will we ever know *our* destiny when we have so little identification with *God's* destiny for the nations?

It certainly is good to pray, "Lord, what is Your will for my life?" But even this can be a self-absorbed prayer. It is far better to pray, "Lord, what is Your will for my *generation?* How do You want my life to fit into Your plan for my times?" Pursuing *God's* purposes, not our own, is the path to personal fulfillment.

Jesus was not kidding when He warned that those who would be self-protective in His kingdom are actually the most at risk: "For whoever desires to save his life will lose it, but whoever loses his life for My sake and the gospel's will save it" (Mark 8:35). Today we talk in terms of self-fulfillment and self-actualization. Not so long ago, Christians spoke of self-sacrifice. Ironically, those earlier generations of Christians ended up a lot more self-fulfilled and self-actualized than are many Christians today! Why? Because they thought Jesus actually meant it when He said that a person truly "finds" his or her life only in laying it down for Christ and for the gospel.

Missionary and writer Amy Carmichael often referred to Christ's last command as "the unrepealed commission." But even the Great Commission must vie for "equal time" in the multi-cause calendars of our church programs today. And the intrinsically confrontational nature of missions makes this greatest of all issues an unwelcome guest in many circles. The whole theology of missions "acts as a gadfly in the house of theology," writes David Bosch, "creating unrest and resisting complacency, opposing every ecclesiastical impulse to self-preservation, every desire to stay what we are, every inclination toward provincialism . . . "[1]

There must be a radical redistribution of our priorities. James warned, "To him who knows to do good and does not do it, to him it is sin" (James 4:17). As a little boy in Sunday school, I learned that there were *sins of omission* (what we should do but don't do), and that these omitted actions were just as displeasing to God as *sins of commission* (what we do but should not do). But recently in my morning devotions I was arrested by the context of that verse. James had just warned against arrogantly pronouncing that "we'll do some long-term planning, and then we'll go into our target city and make some serious money" (my paraphrase). James cautioned that we ought to say, "If the Lord wants us to, we will live and do this or that." So far, so good.

How will we ever know *our* destiny when we have so little identification with *God's* destiny for the nations?

But then I was smacked with his conclusion. "Therefore . . . " (that's what I hadn't seen before). *Therefore,* in light of the fact that the best-laid plans of men can and do evaporate . . . *Therefore,* since our life is no sturdier or longer than a mist . . . (v. 14). *"Therefore,* to him who knows to do good and does not do it, to him it is sin."

The message is unmistakable. Has God told you to do something? Are you aware of something good you ought to be doing for His name? Then why are you sitting on it, as if you had an infinity of time? Get up and do it! Now! If you don't, you are blatantly sinning because you are presuming on a future that is not necessarily yours. The *one moment* you can really "claim" is this one.

It is time for all this pathetic navel-gazing to stop! We must refocus—off our purpose and onto God's purpose, off our own needs and onto the needs of others. William Booth, founder of The Salvation Army, was consumed with a passion for Jesus and a desire to lift others in His name. A forerunner of the Internet in Booth's day was the telegraph. A wealthy philanthropist once offered to telegraph one of Booth's sermons worldwide. Booth excitedly accepted the offer.

"There's one stipulation," the philanthropist cautioned. "Your sermon can only be one word long."

General Booth was quick to comply. Here is his masterpiece, one-word sermon:

Others.

What a fantastic message! William Booth took seriously Paul's admonition in Philippians 2:4–11 (NLT):

**Don't think only about your own affairs, but
be interested in others, too, and what they are
doing. Your attitude should be the same that
Christ Jesus had. Though he was God, he did
not demand and cling to his rights as God. He
made himself nothing; he took the humble
position of a slave and appeared in human
form. And in human form he obediently humbled himself even further by dying a criminal's
death on the cross. Because of this, God raised
him up to the heights of heaven and gave him
a name that is above every other name, so that
at the name of Jesus every knee will bow, in
heaven and on earth and under the earth, and
every tongue will confess that Jesus Christ is
Lord, to the glory of God the Father.**

A Korean Christian once said to me, "We are very grateful to Americans for bringing the gospel to us. For many years you carried the torch of world evangelization. But you have dropped the torch—and the Korean church proudly picks it up." He was not trying to be rude; he was simply comparing the passion levels, as he perceives it, in the Korean and American church. The antidote for lethargy is to get outside of ourselves and embrace a greater vision of God and His unflinching determination to receive glory from every people and nation.

But lethargy is not our only challenge.

STREAMLINING THE STRUCTURE

Is God taunting and teasing thousands of American high school and college students by giving them a burden for unreached peoples with very little possibility of ever actually reaching them?

Obviously not! But to avoid a tidal wave of disappointment, we must see major changes in how we deploy missionaries—and whom we actually send. We may have to discard the "ideal" missionary prototype of the seminary-trained young couple with one or two preschool children. Why? Because God is calling a lot of folks who just do not fit that mold.

No missions conference is complete without a passionate plea to "bring closure" on the Great Commission. But Jay Gary, who directs the Christian Futures Network, is calling on missions leadership to "recognize that it has propagated a scandal of evangelization in raising the rhetoric of closure without changing field deployment priorities among the unreached."[2] That's "missionese" for saying, "Stop kidding the church! You can't fulfill the Great Commission without a whole lot more missionaries actually getting to the remaining unreached peoples!"

Many missions leaders are talking about the need for a new twenty-first-century missionary force of at least two hundred thousand recruits. I personally believe God has *already* spoken to the hearts of at least two hundred thousand believers to invest their lives as missionaries. But when they begin the actual process of trying to go, they begin to feel the squeeze of an archaic bottleneck in the structure.

One of the most pressing missions challenges of this decade is a rapid restructuring that will enable us to quickly deploy fired-up missionary candidates who are still adequately trained. In the past we have made career missionaries jump through too many hoops before we actually send them. The other side of the coin, however, is that they must be adequately prepared, especially emotionally and spiritually, for what lies ahead. Cross-cultural ministry is tougher than it has ever been—not easier. We must find a way both to thoroughly prepare *and* rapidly deploy those God is calling as missionaries.

Patrick Johnstone, who spearheaded research for *Operation World,* is calling for a new level of interdependency between churches, missions agencies and training institutions when it comes to sending workers. He asks, "Should we not rather see the sending as a function of all three structures of the ONE church, working in a mutually accountable partnership?" New training models, especially in the New Apostolic movement, give hope that we can indeed see hot-hearted candidates adequately trained and expeditiously sent.

We can indeed see a "force in the earth" of at least two hundred thousand new missionaries. They will come from many quarters, but there are four eye-popping pools of potential from which God is especially drawing new missionary candidates. Streams of human resources are coming from *youth, the church in developing nations, the African American church* and *women.*

We will look in detail at God's work in missions among youth and the church in developing nations in later chapters. Now let's look at the almost untapped missions reservoir of the African American church. The pressing needs of America's inner cities have kept most African American churches' evangelistic impulses close to home. In very difficult conditions, thousands of African American churches have been a powerful lighthouse, even transforming the very social structures of their neighborhoods. In my city of Dallas, the multiple ministries of powerful churches like Oak Cliff Bible Church and The Potter's House are wonderfully reviving the depressed south part of the city.

African American evangelicals do a far better job than most other evangelicals in maintaining a magnificent balance of compassionate holistic ministry, effusive worship and no-compromise gospel preaching. This is *exactly* what the twenty-first-century missionary force needs to model. And more than ever, African Americans are responding to the Great Commission.

Marilyn Lewis was both a great historian and missions mobilizer among African Americans. Though she died recently of a heart attack, she has seeded Great Commission vision into African American church life that will bear much fruit in this decade. Shortly before her death, she observed:

Today, in the year 2000, we have seen the groundwork laid and are expecting another wide thrust of African American involvement in world evangelization. This period may be called the Great Age of Missions. My belief is that it will be larger and greater than any other involvement of the African American community. It will focus upon all areas of the world—not just Africa. Youth as well as adults will enter into missionary endeavors. This period will witness the increased involvement of short- as well as long-term service. African Americans are now looking seriously at the 10/40 Window, and they are planning how they can be involved. The possibilities are exhilarating.[3]

Then there is the powerful emerging women's movement. Large women's conferences, not only in the United States but also throughout Latin America and other parts of the world, signal a new day for women in missions. Women like Mary

Slessor, Amy Carmichael and Lottie Moon, among many others, gave magnificent leadership to missions in the past. God is raising up a new generation of spiritually dynamic women who, like their predecessors, are ready to bring love and innovation to missions for the twenty-first century.

One of the largest blocs of essentially unreached humanity is the half-billion-plus bloc of Muslim women. There is little hope of reaching most of them by conventional means of evangelism. It would seem that the only hope, certainly the best hope, for reaching them is the compassionate ministries of Christian women. The October 1998 issue of the *YWAM News Digest* observed, "While there are an increasing number of Muslim women pursuing studies and employment, the majority remain isolated from outside contact and hidden within their homes . . . Particularly being separated from male contact, the mobilization of women missionaries is vital."

Women are especially adept at the faithful work that produces great church growth. In 1999, David Yonggi Cho, senior pastor of the world's largest church, reported, "Out of fifty thousand cell leaders in my church, forty-seven thousand are women. I have about six hundred associate pastors. Four hundred of them are women. They are wonderful workers. Without women I don't think I could have built up this big church . . . So, I'm not afraid of having women workers. Because by empowering women we are evangelizing all of Korea."[4]

J. Lee Grady speaks forcefully to the issue of both the necessity and the desirability of masses of female harvesters:

Men cannot fulfill the Great Commission alone—this was never Christ's intention. In fact, when He was describing the way the world would be evangelized, Jesus compared the process to a woman putting leaven in three pecks of meal "until it was all leavened" (Matt. 13:33).

It is interesting that Jesus used a parable involving a woman to describe how the gospel would spread globally from one insignificant city in Israel. I can't help but believe that He was thinking about the vast army of women who would be mobilized in the last days to take His message to the nations. When the job of preaching the gospel to the world is completed, we will discover that women played a major part in the process![5]

CULTURALLY ARROGANT MISSIONS

A recent *National Geographic* survey found that twenty-four million Americans could not locate the United States on a world map. This points to the obvious: For many, their world is much too insular and much too little. The third potential "train wreck" in missions is attitudinal. We Americans are too often embarrassingly paternalistic, even without realizing it. We intrinsically think that we know the best way to do everything, from frying an egg to fixing a flat to "doing church." Consequently, we export what we are comfortable with and often force a young "David" church to wear the "Saul's armor" we feel comfortable in. I cannot tell you the number of times I have winced my way through worship overseas as national believers tried their best to harmonize to Western hymns and sing in four-four time (no doubt in their courteous attempt to make the Americans present feel at home). But when the American "hymn sing" is mercifully over and they begin to sing their indigenous songs of praise, everything changes. Suddenly, the music is no longer disharmonious with their culture. Rather, a unique beauty emerges from their unique songs that no doubt rises as unique incense before the Lord.

My first line of identity is not as an American but as a world Christian. Nevertheless, I cannot hide who I am, nor do I seek to. I am an Anglo-American. I am a beneficiary of the legacy of my ethnicity, including all its sins and triumphs. I am fully aware that indigenous churches and indigenous leaders are at the heart of God's plan for the evangelization of the yet unreached peoples. However, I also understand that the final missions thrust mandates a penetration from outside the culture with the gospel. Nor do I believe God is cruelly teasing thousands of American young people who passionately desire to invest their lives among unreached peoples, no matter how difficult it may be as Americans to actually live and serve among many of these peoples.

You will have to cut the Great Commission out of my Bible for me to believe that my only missions responsibility is to cough up a few hundred bucks each year at a missions conference! Yes, I happen to be a white American, which presents its own set of challenges to actually going to certain areas. But the Great Commission is still in my Bible, and I am bound first by Scripture, not by State Department advisories or visa restrictions. And for the courageous, there really aren't that many closed doors going *in;* it just may prove difficult once you are in to get *out.*

There is still a place for career missionaries from America and other Western nations. But there is no place for any American missionary who wears the grave clothes of colonialism, provincialism or paternalism. The new role of American missionaries is as the junior partner, strengthening the hands and affirming the vision of the church in developing nations and partnering with our brothers and sisters worldwide to ensure "a church for every people and the gospel for every person."

A major twenty-first-century missions challenge is to contextualize the gospel without distorting or diluting it. Don Richardson is right—God has prepared every culture for the gospel and the gospel for every culture.[6] Our great challenge is to be sensitized both to the Holy Spirit and the culture we

38

are trying to reach. Somewhere within that culture there is a key that will unlock their hearts. The art of missions—and the heart of missions—is in finding that key.

TO HELL AND BACK

By far the greatest challenge to missions in this decade is the-ological. If we "derail" theologically, it could take another century to rebuild a solid biblical track underneath the church. Our theological battle is on several fronts, but the most pressing is the deafening silence regarding the creeping universalism that is increasingly present among evangelicals.

Yet somewhere deep in our hearts, we know there must be a day of reckoning. Many futurists fear that as bloody as the nineties were, they were only a prelude to a far greater blood-bath in this decade. Should not all of humanity be ashamed that the world's sworn promise never again to witness another holocaust has been shattered in less than fifty years in Bosnia? Do we not intrinsically know that, outside the lift of regeneration, we are all capable of the most despicable acts? Is there not an innate cry for justice—and an equally intense cry that we seem incapable of effecting justice in our fallen world? Do we not hope against hope that there is coming a day when a holy God will exact both matchless grace and perfect judgment?

Eternal matters often seem irrelevant to a generation bap-tized in hedonism and existentialism. Yet in the deep recesses of our hearts, we know we must face the issue. "Hell is the most offensive and least acceptable of all Christian doctrines," writes David Pawson. "We try to ignore it, but it won't go away. We attempt to explain it away, but it keeps coming back. Better to face the truth, even if it hurts."

I see a catastrophic "train wreck" ahead if we speed to the nations and pay little attention to whether or not the doctrinal tracks supporting us are trustworthy. It is my deep conviction that the number one theological crisis facing evangelicals in the first quarter of this century is what we really believe about eternal judgment. I agree with Pawson that "the recovery of this neglected truth is vital to the health of Christ's body and essential to the task of completing the evangelization of the nations."[7]

We face a disturbing anomaly today: There are many Christians who are excited about missions, but they are not sure they believe in eternal judgment for non-Christians. This is tantamount to carrying a great cause on a weak foundation; eventually, the cause will topple because of wobbly underpinnings.

I do not pretend this is an easy issue. It is a very emotionally uncomfortable subject. Perhaps that's why most people—and most preachers—avoid it. Since the subject is so volatile and the stakes are so high, we must resort not to our own opinions but to the objectivity of Scripture and the words of Jesus Himself.

Jesus spoke far more often of hell than He did of heaven. Our Lord said, "Wide is the gate and broad is the way that leads to destruction, and there are many who go in by it" (Matt. 7:13). Think how "politically incorrect" such a statement is. Jesus' focus was *rescuing souls,* not *protecting feelings.* The Greek word for *destruction* is *apoleia,* clearly a reference to eternal perdition.

Paul wrote pointedly, under the inspiration of the Holy Spirit, of a day " . . . when the Lord Jesus is revealed from heaven with His mighty angels, in flaming fire taking vengeance on those who do not know God, and on those who do not obey the gospel of our Lord Jesus Christ" (2 Thess. 1:7–8). Note carefully and soberly what he says next: "These shall be punished with everlasting destruction from the presence of the Lord and from the glory of His power" (v. 9). No amount of theological spin can make those words say anything else. In the original Greek, "everlasting destruction" means . . . *everlasting destruction.* The eminent church father Augustine concurred: "Our friends who long to get rid of eternal punishment should cease to argue against God and instead obey God's commands while there is still time."

Chuck Colson reminds us of this:

The doctrine of hell is historic Christian orthodoxy. God is a God of love, but he is also a God of justice, and justice requires both heaven (reward for righteousness) and hell (reward for unrighteousness). This divine judgment may sound harsh and inhumane, but the reality of hell is what makes our choices significant and what grants us full human dignity. For if our actions had no ultimate consequences, they would be meaningless. Furthermore, there would be no final moral accountability and therefore no reason for acting morally, which in turn means there would be no basis for a civilized society.[8]

Then there is the well-intentioned question that always crops up in any discussion of missions theology: "What about those who have never heard? Are they saved if they don't hear the gospel?" One of the best responses was given by Charles Spurgeon. When asked if the unreached are saved if they don't hear the gospel, he replied, "The bigger question is, are *we* saved if we don't passionately desire to get the gospel to them?"

At the end of the Lausanne Congress on World Evangelization convened in 1974, there was a passionate commitment to carry the gospel to the ends of the earth. Church planting surged ahead on the twin engines to bring God glory and to rescue the perishing. Evangelicals were clear in both their vision and their theology. Such is not the case today. Missionary statesman Robertson McQuilkin warns:

The most critical issue for missions in the 21st
century is theological. Are those who have never
heard of Christ's saving grace certainly lost? If
there is any question about this, the heroic sacrifices of missionaries in the 19th and 20th centuries will not be forthcoming in the 21st. The
surprise is that few would have thought, in 1974,
that such would become a major theological issue
among those calling themselves evangelical.[9]

Yes, the *highest* motive for missions is the honor of Jesus
Christ and God's global glory, not the threat of eternal punishment for unbelievers. I am quick to admit that an inspiration to "evangelize the heathen" has sometimes led to
simplistic methods and gravely embarrassing cultural mistakes in missions history. Nevertheless, David Pawson is
right when he states that "missionary strategists who consider that a more mature approach can do without such
inspiration have yet to prove that this stimulates greater, or
even equal, zeal."[10] McQuilkin presses the point:

Is God loving? Yes, God is good, and that is
why men are lost. In love He created a being in
His own image, not a robot programmed to
respond as the Maker designed. In creating
such a being to freely love and be loved, God
risked the possibility of such a being rejecting
His love in favor of independence or even self-
love. Humankind did, in fact, choose this
option. Still true to His character, God provided
a way back even though the cost was terrible.
But the way back must not violate the image of
God in man and must not force an obedient
response. Rather, the God of love chooses to
wait lovingly for the response of love. Those
who wish to reject Him may do so.[11]

There are new minefields in this new millennium that require new urgency from us. "If there are indeed 3,884 billion unsaved individuals destined for eternal separation from God," writes pastor Larry Stockstill, "our lives become bigger and more significant than utility bills and relational problems."[12]

Antecedent to any great move of God, somebody somewhere has been weeping instead of sleeping, agonizing before God for the lost. Glorious harvest is promised to those who have sown in tears. "Those who plant in tears will harvest with shouts of joy. They weep as they go to plant their seed, but they sing as they return with the harvest" (Ps. 126:5–6, NLT).

THE ONE AND ONLY

Larry King, the talk-show host, was once asked whom, of all people who have ever lived, he would most want to interview. King replied that his choice would be Jesus Christ and that he would ask Him just one question: "Are You indeed virgin born?" "The answer to that question," King said, "would explain history for me."[13] If Christ's virgin birth is a reality, then a new way of seeing erupts, free from the constrictions of naturalism.

The uniqueness of Jesus as God the Son is the very core of our message and, therefore, our mission. *Who is Jesus and what will you do with Him?* This is the Great Divide, the all-important issue.

Almost every religion has high regard for Jesus. But whether or not He is the one and only redeemer—or if humans even *need* a redeemer—is where biblical Christianity parts company with every other faith. *Newsweek* correspondent Kenneth L. Woodward put the issue of who Jesus is and what His cross is all about as the central abrasive issue:

Clearly, the cross is what separates the Christ
of Christianity from every other [viewpoint

regarding] Jesus. In Judaism there is no
precedent for a Messiah who dies, much less
as a criminal as Jesus did. In Islam, the story of
Jesus' death is rejected as an affront to Allah
himself. Hindus can accept only a Jesus who
passes into peaceful samadhi, a yogi who
escapes the degradation of death. "The figure
of the crucified Christ," says Buddhist Thich
Nhat Hanh, "is a very painful image to me. It
does not contain joy or peace, and this does
not do justice to Jesus." There is, in short, no
room in other religions for a Christ who
experiences the full burden of mortal
existence—and hence there is no reason to
believe in him as the divine Son whom the
Father resurrected from the dead.[14]

By contrast, this cross—this sacrifice—that is so repugnant
to others is attractive and precious to us who believe. It is at
the same time the ultimate tragedy and the ultimate triumph.
As Ravi Zacharias observes, "This is the moment toward
which all of history had been moving and by which history
would be forevermore defined."[15]

Those who wish to escape Jesus and His cross find it is too
colossal to evade. This is seen in Woodward's quote. Whether
or not people believe in Him, they are compelled to *deal with
Him*. Zacharias continues, "Those who hated Him, He loved.
Those who killed Him wanted to be rid of Him. By allowing
Himself to be killed, He made it possible for them to live.
The crucifixion of Jesus was the embodied expression of
rebellion against God...He came to lay down His life so that
the very ones who killed Him, who represented all of us,
could be forgiven because of the price that He paid in the
hell of a world that does not recognize His voice."[16]

It is this towering God in flesh who magnetically elicits

our worship. How do you describe Him? John R. Mott gave it a pretty good try:

In Christ, the central figure of the ages and of the eternities, we have one other than all the rest—other than the ancient sages and holy men of Hinduism, other than Buddha or Mohammed, other than Moses and St. Paul, other than Gandhi and Kagawa. Yes, other than them and other than all the rest. There He stands—erect among the fallen, strong among the weak, believing among the faithless, clean among the defiled, living among the dead—alive forevermore, therefore the fountainhead of vitality and the generating source of the most profound social changes.[17]

May God save us from disasters of our own making. God grant that we will shake ourselves loose from lethargy and embrace new millennium missions with innovative structures, cultural respect, Holy Spirit anointing and biblical fidelity. There is an emerging generation that will.

The mantle of authority is now passing to a younger generation of leaders who are boldly rising up to their responsibility...Intimacy with Christ coupled with praise and worship are core values. A deep longing for unity among the entire body of Christ compels these young leaders to overcome denominational and doctrinal differences within the evangelical tradition. They want mentoring and input from mature leaders as they work in unity to complete the Great Commission. We, therefore, covenant together to support these emerging leaders whom God has raised up, to encourage them in their dreams and to make room for their gifts, ideas and initiatives.
—THE MILLENNIAL MANIFESTO:
COVENANTING FOR THE TWENTY-FIRST CENTURY

You are only a teenager for seven years. If you survive, you may well be an adult ten times longer. Give God the tithe of your teenage years, and He will give you an open heaven for the rest of your life.
—GREG JOHNSON

My heart is bursting, Lord,
To tell of all You've done,
Of how You changed my life
And wiped away the past.
I wanna shout it out,
From every rooftop sing,
For now I know that God is for me,
Not against me!
—"THE HAPPY SONG" BY MARTIN SMITH[1]

THREE

The Global Jesus Movement

Before I formed you in the womb I knew you . . . I ordained you a prophet to the nations.
—JEREMIAH 1:5

And it shall come to pass afterward that I will pour out My Spirit on all flesh; your sons and your daughters shall prophesy, your old men shall dream dreams, your young men shall see visions.
—JOEL 2:28–29

T he moment I stepped on the Capitol Mall in Washington I began to weep. In a sea of three hundred fifty thousand people (mostly young people), I found myself in a square yard sanctuary of personal revival.² Crying gave way to sobbing as I interceded for this generation. Intermittent waves crashed over me—waves of repentance for my generation's sins against this younger generation, pleas for mercy on this new generation and deep gratitude that I had lived to see this day. This God encounter went on for forty-five minutes.

Sensing something of the magnitude of this event, I had

47

flown from Dallas just to be there and pray. All day long rushes of gratitude swept over me. I recalled how as a college student I had taken part in Explo '72, what many believe was the zenith of the Jesus Movement. Now, almost thirty years later, I was privileged to see it happening all over again. The Hebrew word *chabod* describes a literal weight when God displays His glory. So, to coin both a Hebrew and a hippie term, the Jesus Movement was *heavy*, but what we are seeing now is even *heavier.*

Psalm 110 is a prophetic pronouncement of the Messiah's rule over the nations. This psalm assures God's people that His enemies will become His footstool. Then there's the thrilling promise, "Your people shall be volunteers in the day of Your power; in the beauties of holiness, from the womb of the morning, You have the dew of Your youth" (Ps. 110:3).

What a promise! When God reveals His glory, His people will volunteer as carriers of His glory! But exactly who are these "troops arrayed in holy majesty"? (Ps. 110:3, NIV). The answer: "Your young men and women will come to You like the dew of the morning!"

This verse is showing us a picture of how God will work in the last days. Dew is pure and refreshing. Even in seasons without rain, God lovingly irrigates the needy earth with His reviving dew. Just so, even when the rains of revival are absent, God will refresh the world with the dew of youth who are His to command. The *dew* that is His will bring the *due* that is His.

Dew shows up in the morning; it comes when the night is past. God is saying that the long night is over, and the parched earth will now be refreshed. When the youthful troops report for duty—when God receives young troops arrayed in holy majesty—it signals that refreshing has come. Night has surrendered to dawn.

As I stood on the Mall in Washington, before my eyes I was watching God call out "the dew of youth"—His young, volunteer troops. As His glory descended on them, He was clothing them in holy majesty. They are part of a twenty-first-century continuum. In fact, the awesome account of the advance of Christianity is essentially the story of how God uses His willing troops—youth from every nation who are coming to Him like the dew.

JESUS PEOPLE REVISITED

Each day heaven's new heroes are writing new chapters of bravery. Now with the finish line in sight of "a church for every people and the gospel for every person,"[3] once again God is looking for His "first-choice" runners—young men and women with a passion to see every nation and people bring honor to the Son of God.

God calls people of every age, but His eye is especially on

The *dew* that is His will bring the *due* that is His.

youth. Throughout the Bible when God had a big job to do He often called on a young person. When it was time to silence a blaspheming giant, God chose a teenager named David. When God wanted literally to cut off idolatry at the knees, He chose a young man named Gideon (who had to be persuaded by an angel that he was a "mighty man of valor"). When a nation needed prophetic guidance, God tapped a no-compromise young man named Daniel. When it was time for God to put on skin and send His Son, He chose a willing teenage virgin named Mary.

A PURE FAITH

Yes, God often reserves the really great assignments for young people. It is not hard to see why. For one thing, most Christian young people have a *pure faith*. The venom of skepticism and unbelief hasn't poisoned their spiritual bloodstream. God is presently injecting many twenty-first-century leaders with the missions addiction. Some of them are reading this book.

Many qualities go into the making of a leader—some

If you completely follow Jesus, you will never lack for adventure!

beyond the control of a developing leader. But the single most important quality of spiritual leadership—faith—is entirely in your court. You will determine how much faith you have—and how much faith you will exercise. You and you alone will make the choice of how much and how radically you will believe God.

DISCONTENTED WITH THE STATUS QUO

Youth have always been *very willing to defy the status quo*. That's good! There is a lot that needs changing. Hudson Taylor was in his early twenties when he arrived in China. He met stiff resistance from veteran missionaries when he bravely chose to adopt Chinese habits of dress and diet. Yet his farsighted strategy was decades ahead of his time, and it allowed Taylor to capture the hearts of the Chinese in an unprecedented way.

RISK-TAKERS

Youth enjoy *taking risks*. Toby McKeehan, from dc Talk and co-writer of the song *Jesus Freak*, agrees:

This generation is into extremes. There are extreme sports, and Hollywood is throwing extremes at us. I believe that Christians will live up to these extremes because that is what the culture calls for. As believers, we need to be just as potent.[4]

One key reason why God so greatly uses young people is that they simply do not know what the parameters are. If there's a huge assignment, they just do it—and find out that it was *impossible* later!

If you are a young person reading these words, I promise one thing: *If you completely follow Jesus, you will never lack for adventure!* C. S. Lewis, in his great novel *The Lion, the Witch and the Wardrobe*, tells the enthralling story of four children who go through the portals of a wardrobe into the enchanted kingdom of Narnia. There they are enmeshed in the drama between the White Witch and Aslan, the lion, for rule over the kingdom. Aslan, of course, is a type of Christ, and Lewis's fictional stories mirror a real-life epic that is being played out on a global scale. One of the children, Lucy, asks Mr. Beaver, a loyal follower of the lion, if Aslan is safe. "Safe?" replied Mr. Beaver. "Who said anything about safe? 'Course he isn't safe. But he's good. He's the king, I tell you."[5]

ABLE TO EMPATHIZE

Another reason God uses young people is because of their great *ability to empathize.* Violence, fractured families and demolished dreams have left many young people very familiar with pain and loss. But God steps in and uses that very brokenness to bring healing to many. The Christian band Delirious? sings:

Is it true today, that when people stand
With the fire of God and the truth in hand,
We'll see miracles, we'll see angels sing,
We'll see broken hearts making history?
Yes, it's true.[6]

God uses brokenhearted people because they feel the pain of a fractured world that is separated from God. Recently I was with three other presidents of missions organizations. As we shared our backgrounds, we discovered that each of us had experienced a major family tragedy when we were teenagers. Bob Pierce was such a man. He cried his way home from seeing firsthand the aftermath of the Korean War. On the way home, Pierce wrote in the flyleaf of his Bible, "Let my heart be broken by the things that break the heart of God." It was one of those strong, simple prayers that set movements in motion. He focused his personal pain redemptively and founded two great Christian ministries, World Vision and Samaritan's Purse.

"Why should anyone hear the gospel twice until everyone has heard it once?"

When families disintegrate and hopes evaporate, many young people experience not only a broken heart but also rejection. Young people today feel enormous rejection, particularly from performance-driven adults who are vicariously trying to atone for their own failures by forcing their children to live in pressure cookers. In fact, it may be that there is a far more cavernous *generation gap* between adults and youth today than there was thirty-five years ago when that term was first coined. But Jesus always hotly pursues the rejected. Better than anyone else, He knows the pain this generation is going through. He was "despised and rejected by men, a Man of sorrows and acquainted with grief" (Isa. 53:3).

Maybe that is why teenagers love Him so ardently. The depth of love for Jesus and the identification with His broken heart that is evident among many youth who do not "look right" is an embarrassing indictment to those who would worship from a distance. The complacent want to label this level of devotion as *madness*. But Winkey Pratney notes:

The world has never been moved by the mild or

the moderate ... The choice we are presented
with in the closing days of history may not be
between the mad and the sane, but between
holy and unholy madness ... Hence, God is
recruiting from the ranks of the rejected.[7]

Nobody can identify with the woundedness of this young generation better than young people themselves. That's why they are the natural evangelists to their friends and why, since the Columbine tragedy, American high schools have been aflame with bold witnesses for Christ.

RECOGNIZE INJUSTICES

Most young people also have a *keen sense of injustice.* By their words and actions, young people are crying out, "That's not fair!" In Oswald J. Smith's classic book *The Passion for Souls,* he issues this gut-wrenching polemic set against the backdrop of the Western church's indifference: "Why should anyone hear the gospel twice until everyone has heard it once?" The injustice of that reality lit a fire in my heart. And it is this same deeply felt inequity coupled with the unbridled evangelistic passion of youth today that is producing great spiritual harvest.

JUST BEGINNING LIFE

Finally, young people *have their whole lives ahead of them.* It is in their teens and twenties that most people make the three most important choices in life—a master, a mission and a mate. Someone has well said that any evangelism targeting those beyond high school is more *salvage* than *evangelism!* May God help today's embattled youth to choose wisely. The impact they make for Jesus while they are young can be built upon for the rest of their lives.

The Jesus Movement was a precious, gentle breeze of God's Spirit that literally rescued a generation of youth on the brink of destruction. Back then many of us thought that *radical* meant wearing your hair long and strumming love songs to Jesus. Today's "long hairs" are sometimes young Nazarites who have taken a literal vow before God for revival!

Today's young "Jesus freaks" are truly radical! Teenage girls in China head underground networks of hundreds of house churches. Last year a seventeen-year-old student in India was used by God to raise a woman from the dead.[8] Thousands of South Korean students are poised to carry the gospel to their northern neighbor, the repressive nation of North Korea. I have personally seen thousands of Brazilian young people weep before God in deep commitment as they surrender their lives to reach the remaining peoples in the 10/40 Window.

God has not overlooked this young generation. They have been singled out for great things. This precious, broken-hearted generation, battered and victimized by the sins of adults, is getting the missions addiction! They will be history makers. Yes, it's true.

A CLOUD OF HOPE

Today's youth are forcing a more rigorous (and more biblical) faith walk on the church. Their faith has been heat-tempered by high school martyrs and summers given voluntarily in ministry among the world's most needy. George Barna has issued some statistics regarding evangelical young people that are pretty dismal, including these:

■ Only 9 percent of born-again teenagers are certain of the existence of absolute moral truth.

■ Only 44 percent of born-again teenagers claim that they are "absolutely committed to the Christian faith."

■ Although two-thirds of all teenagers say they know all the basic teachings and principles of the Christian faith, two-thirds of them reject the existence of Satan, three-fifths reject the existence of the Holy Spirit and half believe that Jesus sinned during His lifetime.[9]

But youth also are the most hopeful sign in the church today.

For one thing, this generation represents the *first generation of teenage martyrs in America. Gen Y* kids know that if they pray for fellow students at "See You at the Pole," they could be gunned down like the students in Paducah, Kentucky. They know that if they share their faith openly, they could be shot like the courageous Christians at Columbine. They are even aware that if they just go to a church youth meeting, they could be blown away like the kids at Wedgwood Baptist Church in Fort Worth. In other words, even in America there is a price to pay if you love Jesus.

This costly Christianity is producing young people who are *outspoken witnesses for Christ.* They boldly share their faith, knowing there will be consequences. Because my generation has wimped out, young people have had to carry the battle and become the conscience for freedom of religious expression in America. For publicly declaring "that name," they are often castigated, not just by students but especially by intimidated (and convicted?) adults.

The name of Jesus is ringing through the halls of high schools and colleges, and unbelievers are uncomfortable, to say the least. They are scared spitless of "that name." Unbelievers seem to perceive its power intrinsically. No doubt that is why, even as I write, a landmark case is going to the Supreme Court that will decide whether public schools and government agencies can refuse to allow religious groups to use their buildings to conduct religious-oriented programs.[10]

As Winkey Pratney points out, "Hell sometimes seems to know better than the church the critical nature of the hour." The average age of conversion today in the United States is fifteen years old, and 80 percent of all conversions take place by the age of twenty-four.[11] Hence the frenzied attempt of many postmoderns to eradicate Jesus' name from the public arena. But be encouraged—Jesus is too large to ever be silenced. His name "will be great among the nations" (Mal. 1:11, NAS).

This young American generation is also unique because they are *more missions conscious* than any previous generation. Guess what? There were more American teenagers on missions trips last summer than ever in the history of this nation! That is the single most hopeful sign in the American church today. Those who have served on missions teams come back with greater compassion and a broadened worldview. Once stretched, their hearts can never go back to their previous size. Most of all, they contract the missions addiction. A missions serum gets injected into their spiritual bloodstream, and they are never again "normal," laid-back Christians. They have been "ruined" for mediocrity! These missions-savvy teenagers and twenty-somethings work as good leaven throughout their local churches, kneading a vision for God's global glory into the entire church.

From middle schools to college campuses, God is working by His Spirit, producing a new force of millennial missionaries. To be sure, there are serious challenges. Of the fifteen million new college students, only 20 percent claim any sort of relationship with Christ. And, while Gen-Xers and millennials are spiritually hungry, they are also often biblically illiterate and tend to value relevancy over truth.

Still, something wonderful is happening. Already this youth awakening is more potent than the Jesus Movement thirty years ago. But here's the exciting difference: We are only in the early stages of this new, global Jesus Movement. What we are seeing now in Acquire the Fire weekends, Life Challenge meetings, The Call DC and One Day conferences is already more awesome than the Jesus Movement at its peak.

A major difference between this move and the move of the seventies is that the stakes are much higher today. Then, out-

A missions serum gets injected into their spiritual bloodstream, and they are never again "normal," laid-back Christians.

siders laughed at "Jesus freaks." Now they shoot them. Some adults still think they can live in an insular world where everybody is basically "nice." Young people know better. They have counted the cost, and they are willing to pay. They agree with Philip Yancey, who said:

Only a life given away for love's sake is a life worth living. To bring His point home, God shows us a man who gave His life away to the extent of dying a national disgrace without a penny in the bank or a friend to His name. In terms of men's wisdom, He was a perfect fool, and anybody who thinks he can follow Him without making something like the same fool of himself is laboring under not a cross but a delusion.[12]

This new, sold-out generation follows in a noble train.

ON THE BACKS OF TWENTY-SOMETHINGS

What do Mary Slessor, Hudson Taylor and Cameron Townsend share in common? They were all impacting nations and changing missions paradigms before they were thirty years old.

In fact, the advance of the gospel throughout church

history has generally been on the backs (and backpacks) of twenty-somethings. On-fire young people today are following in a train of faith that is centuries long.

The average age was twenty-seven at the Moravian meeting at Herrnhut on August 13, 1727, when at a communion service the presence of Christ was so overwhelming that it launched a prayer meeting that continued nonstop for one hundred years.

In the first era of missionary advance, God sent William Carey, not yet thirty years old, to defy a complacent English church and challenge believers to see a bigger world. This young pastor dared Christians of his day to "expect great things from God and attempt great things for God!" God is putting that same impassioned faith in the hearts of His young firebrands today.

In the second era it was again young men and women, including Hudson Taylor, David Livingstone and Mary Slessor, who made the difference in their generation. As the third era dawned, young, fresh thinkers such as Cameron Townsend and Donald McGavran again changed the course of missions.

The golden chain of the gospel's advance has always been forged by young people. Nikolaus von Zinzendorf, who would later give leadership to the Moravians, was ten years old when he determined his lifelong purpose would be to preach Christ to the world. When he was sixteen, Zinzendorf joined with five other teenagers to form a school prayer group in Germany. It grew into a revival prayer movement that swept Europe! Zinzendorf lived in a time of fervent nationalism. But his love and loyalty to Jesus was so encompassing that he said, "That land is henceforth my country which most needs the gospel."

Youthful Baptist pastor Charles Simeon challenged Cambridge students in the 1790s toward missions and sparked a student Christian movement that has impacted that campus to the present day.

The Global Jesus Movement

Across the Atlantic, the impromptu Haystack Prayer Meeting at Williams College in 1806 launched the American missions movement. Samuel Mills, one of the students at that historic gathering, galvanized a student missions movement that reached seventy American campuses. Mills died at thirty-five off the coast of Liberia on a missionary voyage. But in his young life he helped form America's first missionary society and the American Bible Society.

David Livingstone was a teenager when he heard Robert Moffat, a missionary to Africa, say that at dusk he could look inland and "see the smoke of a thousand villages without the gospel." Livingstone changed his life's focus and determined to get the gospel to those villages.

In 1850 teenager Hudson Taylor committed his life to serve Christ in China. In the same decade, David Livingstone preached at Cambridge, touching off a second missions blaze from the still-smoldering ashes of the evangelistic fire Charles Simeon lit sixty years earlier. In 1858, Inter-Varsity Christian Fellowship began at Cambridge, tracing its roots to Livingstone's impact on the campus.

Also in 1858, Luther Wishard suggested a summer conference for students to evangelist D. L. Moody. Wishard's sister prophesied that there would be one hundred missionary volunteers from the conference. The next year, the first student missions conference convened at Mount Hermon. After missionary A. T. Pierson's challenge to "the evangelization of the world in this generation," exactly one hundred students pledged their lives to become missionaries. This became the genesis of the Student Volunteer Movement, which would eventually see over twenty thousand American young people go as missionaries.

Once again, a missions spirit hit Cambridge when D. L. Moody preached there in 1882. Among those converted at Moody's meetings was a young cricket player named C. T. Studd. He would voluntarily give up his inherited fortune to finance his missions work and the founding of the World Evangelization Crusade (WEC).

As the fire finally began to play out in the Student

They just never got over the grace of God. It captured them and then propelled them to the nations.

Volunteer Movement, fifty-three students met in 1936 in North Carolina, asking God to renew missions passion among young people. The result was the Student Foreign Missions Fellowship, which Jim Elliot would head at Wheaton College a decade later. Also resulting from this meeting, InterVarsity began triennial student missions conventions, which have become the far-reaching Urbana Missions Conferences. The most recent Urbana conference in December 2000 was attended by 18,730 delegates, mostly college students and high school seniors. Since 1946, almost two hundred thousand students have attended this conference, and many thousands have responded to the call to missionary service.[13]

Youth-lit fires continued to spread. Billy Graham and Torrey Johnson, a young evangelist and pastor, formed Youth for Christ in 1944. Soon its impact was being felt worldwide. In 1951, a young seminary student named Bill Bright launched Campus Crusade for Christ.

In 1956, twenty-nine-year-old Jim Elliot and four other young missionaries were martyred in an attempt to plant the gospel among the remote Huaorani (Auca) of Ecuador. In Christian college chapel services, or privately as students read the cover story of their martyrdom in *Life* magazine, hundreds volunteered to take their place. Elliot's young widow, Elisabeth, would courageously go back with her baby daughter and Rachael Saint, sister of martyred Nate Saint.

They succeeded in planting a living church among the Huaorani that is thriving today.

In some respects, missions seemed to go underground in the 1960s with rising tides of nationalism and America's pre-occupation with Vietnam and domestic violence. But God was again preparing young hearts to launch yet another wave of missions expansion. Fuller Seminary's School of World Missions, Oral Roberts University and Christ For The Nations were all birthed in that turbulent decade.

Around the same time, Loren Cunningham envisioned masses of youth going around the world with the gospel. He saw them as perhaps the greatest untapped resource for missions. Cunningham also realized that many missions agencies at that time were either unable or unwilling to give these young people significant, short-term missions experiences. In response, he founded Youth With A Mission (YWAM), opening the way for thousands to experience missions first-hand. As one young man observed, "Loren Cunningham deregulated missions."

Then came the Jesus Movement. Although the movement itself was not overtly missionary, in my travels to over fifty nations I frequently meet "Jesus people" who came to Christ in the Jesus Movement and have spent the ensuing decades in grateful service for Him. They just never got over the grace of God. It captured them and then propelled them to the nations.

The "golden chain" continues. Ron and Katie Luce, young married students at Oral Roberts University in the 1980s, dreamed of igniting a fire for missions in a whole generation of youth. The result is Teen Mania. Twenty-six times each year thousands of teenagers literally "acquire the fire." Somehow an evangelistic crusade, revival meeting and pyrotechnic missions conference are wrapped into one awesome weekend! Each summer, thousands get their first taste of missions through their own church outreaches or through groups like Teen Mania, Teen Missions and dozens of other youth missions outreaches that are proliferating. The result is that today's Christian young people have a more serious missions addiction than any previous generation!

THE GRAND PRIZE

Some time ago God began to speak to me about this generation. He assured my heart that there would be another sweep of His Spirit that would usher hundreds of thousands of young people into the kingdom and out to the ends of the earth.

Now as I open my heart in Bible schools and youth missions conferences around the world, I am finding enormous

Today's Christian young people have a more serious missions addiction than any previous generation!

receptivity in a generation hungry for God and hungry for fathers. As I meet with thousands of young men and women whom God is calling, I am discovering young Christian leaders who are stellar models of attractive, holy passion for Jesus in this new era. I am honored to stand by the side of these young missions addicts in the battle to make Jesus Christ known, loved and worshiped in the twenty-first century.

One hundred years ago visionary missions statesman John R. Mott made a prophetic plea:

In view of the constraining memories of the cross of Christ and the love wherewith He hath loved us, let us rise and resolve, at whatever cost of self-denial, that live or die, we shall live or die for the evangelization of the world in our day.[14]

With all my heart I believe he foresaw this generation. Toughened by persecution, broken for the lost, smitten with love for Jesus, they will have the obedience, courage and determination to break open the final frontiers.

Many refer to this young generation as the *Joshua generation* in missions.[15] Even in the new praise and worship styles, this generation is blaring the message that, like Joshua and his young army, they will not be denied their spiritual inheritance. God will have "the dew of the youth" of all nations! And He is calling His sons and daughters from the ends of the earth:

I will bring your children from the east and gather you from the west. I will say to the north, "Give them up!" and to the south, "Do not hold them back." Bring my sons from afar and my daughters from the ends of the earth— everyone who is called by my name.
—Isaiah 43:5–7, niv

The young millennials are also sometimes referred to as "the terminal generation." I believe this is true, but it is an unwitting prophecy instead of a stigma of doom. I believe it is a prophetic declaration going back to the root Latin word *terminus,* meaning "fulfillment or completion of a season of time." I am convinced that God is going to give this generation the grand prize for which twenty centuries of believers have prayed, worked and dreamed—closure on the Great Commission!

MENTORING THE PASSION

God is not teasing or mocking thousands of youth by putting the yet unreached peoples so forcibly on their hearts. He will show them creative ways to get the gospel to the remaining peoples. But the passion of youth does need mentoring. Wise adults need to be skilled encouragers who help channel the fire where it can be most effective.

Over ten years ago, in a season of prayer, I felt the Lord promise me that there would be another major move of His Spirit among young people, but this move would be more radical and much more decidedly missions-oriented. Soon after, Ron Luce called and asked if I would serve on the board of directors for Teen Mania. I gladly said yes, knowing in my spirit what was about to break forth.

As one of the directors, I was privileged to be part of the process of Teen Mania's move from Tulsa to their beautiful, four-hundred-acre, east Texas campus. It seems to me much more than mere coincidence that the campus of Teen Mania sits on the very property where Keith Green and his ministry touched an earlier generation for missions. In his hot pursuit after God, Keith Green had contracted the missions addiction. In his last year of ministry he continually pressed American young people to deal with the Great Commission. Keith's final message was a challenge to hands-on missionary involvement. Today that vision is lived out as hundreds of young men and women prepare for Christ's service at Teen Mania's Honor Academy. I believe it is a perfect "torch pass" orchestrated by the Holy Spirit.

What a privilege our generation has of passing the torch of the gospel from one millennium to another! But how do we impart missions passion to today's youth?

AFFIRM YOUTH

First, it is important to *affirm them*. We should be their most ardent cheerleaders. John R. Mott was not only the leading missions statesman of his day, but he was also called the "father of the young people of the world." He had an abiding love and confidence in young people and believed the only hope of continually revitalizing ministries was to place youth in the highest levels of decision-making.

The high level devotion of young radicals is in stark contrast to the painless Christianity espoused by many adults.

As I said earlier, today's youth are forcing a tougher (and more biblical) faith walk on the church—a commitment that is heat-tempered by martyrdom and missions. In short, they are calling us back to mere Christianity. We owe these young people an all-consuming passion: a passion for God's glory in their own lives and in the lives of every people. They will take nothing less.

STRETCH YOUTH

Second, we need to *stretch them*. Self-destructive philosophies are rampant, even among many Christian teenagers. If there is a disconnect between the beauty of their worship

> I am committed to being part of the "Caleb generation" that says, "Give me that mountain! Age is not the issue. There's still more territory to take for His glory."

and the carnality of their lives, this should not go unchallenged. Today's teenagers are used to "in your face" confrontations. Effective youth ministers have learned to issue no-joke, snap-to, wake-up calls to a total life reorientation—moving away from placid, self-serving, pseudo-Christianity and toward the radical discipleship Jesus has always required.

INSPIRE YOUTH

Third, we should *inspire them*. Generations X and Y need to hear the story of how—and why—Jim Elliot never saw his thirtieth birthday. He was barely out of his teens when he scratched in his journal some of the most profound devotional musings of the twentieth century, including, "He is no fool who gives what he cannot keep to gain what he cannot lose." We need to remind teenagers that Mary Slessor was changing the entire social and spiritual landscape of West Africa when she was still in her twenties. They need to know that Chinese teenagers are leading congregations of thousands, and in the last few years, almost one hundred thousand Indian and Korean students have committed their lives for missionary service in the 10/40 Window.

God is once again looking for—and finding—young mavericks who will say yes and believe.

There are plenty of caustic voices in the church who are telling kids today that it can't be done and that world evangelization is a pipe dream. Dear God, deliver me from any identification with them! I am OK with losing my hair, but not my faith! I can live with dimming eyesight, as long as my vision is getting brighter! I am committed to being part of the "Caleb generation" that says, "Give me that mountain! Age is not the issue. There's still more territory to take for His glory."

We don't need to sugarcoat the missions message or minimize the challenge of the remaining peoples. But we should marinate reality in the juices of hope. As mentors to young visionaries, we must never be guilty of preventing youthful dreams from getting airborne. Yes, we can help guide where those dreams will soar, but we must never strap down the wings of vision or creativity. My advice: Never, *never* allow your dreams to be held hostage. Don't let any well-intentioned friend, family member or preacher extract any dream God has put in your heart. Go for it! And if it fails, regroup and go for it again!

We adults must never diss a dream or douse the flames of youthful passion with the waters of doubt. One reason God chose Mary as His instrument for the revelation of God's Son to the world was because of her dangerous, self-sacrificial faith. Not only did Mary believe for great things, but she also believed the word of the Lord for something that had never happened before. Never in history had there been a virgin birth, but a teenager named Mary said yes and believed.

Never in history has there been actual fulfillment of the Great Commission. God is once again looking for—and finding—young mavericks who will say yes and believe.

The great Christian revolutions come not by the discovery of something that was not known before. They happen when somebody takes radically something that was always there.
–H. RICHARD NIEBUHR

It is easier to serve God without a vision, easier to work for God without a call, because then you are not bothered by what God requires; common sense is your guide . . . You will be more leisure-hearted if you never realize the call of God. But if once you receive a commission from Jesus Christ, the memory of what God wants will always come like a goad; you will no longer be able to work for Him on the common-sense basis.
–OSWALD CHAMBERS

Being in the middle of the road is probably the worst thing you can say about anyone.
–PHIL COLLINS

FOUR

Farewell to the Balanced Life

Who makes His angels spirits, His ministers a flame of fire.
—PSALM 104:4

His ever expanding, peaceful government will never end…The
passionate commitment of the Lord Almighty will guarantee this!
—ISAIAH 9:7, NLT

S tanding on Brighton Beach, I looked out toward the European continent and let the crisp sea wash across my face. It was the summer of 1992. At that south England beach I thought back to a very different time but the same place.

It was Brighton Beach, but the year was 1850. Hudson Taylor, still a teenager and only recently converted, surrendered his life to God for China on that same wind-swept, sandy beach. In the aftermath of that experience with God at Brighton, Taylor said, "I feel that I cannot go on living unless I do something for China."

That day Hudson Taylor said farewell to the balanced life.

From that moment on he was driven—driven for God and driven for His glory in China. The ramifications of Taylor's commitment are still rumbling throughout China today. In fact, Ruth Tucker asserts that "no other missionary in nineteen centuries since the apostle Paul has had a wider vision and has carried out a more systematized plan of evangelizing a broad geographical area than Hudson Taylor."[1]

Paul *burned* for Christ's honor, and he was completely convinced that his message would take hold and have a transforming, even explosive, effect on the hearers.

Hudson Taylor had the missions addiction, and he was committed to seeing God's glory revealed to the peoples of China. He was the kind of clear-headed radical T. E. Lawrence had in mind when he observed, "All men dream, but not equally. Those who dream by night in the dusty recesses of their minds wake in the day to find that it was vanity. But the dreamers of the day are dangerous men, for they may act their dream with open eyes, to make it possible."[2]

As the salt water sprayed my face I prayed, "God, do it again. Raise up a new generation of missions addicts who are dreamers of the day."

ANCHORED RADICALS

As with Paul before him, once Hudson Taylor encountered Jesus Christ, his priorities were forever overturned. With Paul he felt that he was a debtor to bring the gospel to those who had not heard it. And with Paul he pursued the vision with white-hot passion. Taylor echoed Paul's heart, "For I have a great sense of obligation to people in our culture and to people in other cultures, to the educated and uneducated alike. So I am eager to come to you in Rome, too, to preach God's Good News" (Rom. 1:14–15, NLT).

The word translated "eager" or "ready" in verse 15 gives us a glimpse into Paul's passion. There are two Greek words meaning "prepared" or "ready." Paul deliberately chose the more pungent word—*prothumos*—which carries the idea of literally being on fire! Not only was Paul prepared, but he also burned to preach the gospel! How tragic that we send people to seminary who are on fire but feel unprepared. Three years later, they feel prepared, but too often the fire has been doused. Let's take a lesson from the apostle Paul. He could run theological circles around any academician, but he also kept the fire!

The word *prothumos* can also mean "to think with a future mind." Paul wasn't just charged up about preaching the gospel; he also saw by faith the effect the gospel would have! As a missionary visionary, Paul saw into the future and envisioned the redeeming effects of the gospel not only on individual lives but also on an entire empire. He craved the privilege of "seeding" the gospel into Rome, knowing that it would, in the end, topple paganism and totally transform the culture.

I am convinced this is a key to understanding how Paul sustained passion, even when he was in the direst circumstances. Paul *burned* for Christ's honor, and he was completely convinced that his message would take hold and have a transforming, even explosive, effect on the hearers. No wonder he said in the next verse, "For I am not ashamed of the gospel of Christ, for it is the power of God to salvation for everyone who believes" (Rom. 1:16).

But this kind of language, much less this kind of passion, is extraneous to many today. To be sure, we thrive on *vision,* but we are repelled by *burden*. We hear much about *destiny* but almost nothing about *dying to self*. We exult *in the joy of the Lord*, but *travail for souls* is foreign to us. Consequently we sometimes succumb to discouragement because we tie our hopes to our circumstances instead of strapping our hopes to the unstoppable power of the gospel.

In the 1960s many hippies claimed to be radicals, but their radicalism was wasted because they cut loose from historic moorings and consequently lost their moral authority. A true radical is one who defies the whims of his times and calls people back to root realities and root causes.

The screaming need today is anchored radicals . . .

- Radicals who are anchored in truth, not conjecture

- Radicals who are anchored in grace, not legalism

- Radicals who are anchored in faith, not skepticism

- Radicals who are anchored in discipline, not indolence

- Radicals who are anchored in history, not fads

- Radicals who are anchored in hope, not despair

Most of all, we need radicals who are anchored in Christ and the assurance of His global glory:

We who have fled to him for refuge can take new courage, for we can hold on to his promise with confidence. This confidence is like a strong and trustworthy anchor for our souls.
—HEBREWS 6:18–19, NLT

TWENTY-FIRST-CENTURY JONAHS

The American church often seems adrift with no place to land and no rock on which to anchor. Look at the shift of focus. No longer is the object God, or even others. The new center of attraction is *self!* Many today are completely unmoved by the fate of the unconverted and wholly disinterested in God's purposes for their generation. Yet the same Christians who yawn with boredom when *evangelism* or *missions* are mentioned are often heated in their denunciations against society's sins.

Hey, don't we get it? Lost people are just acting–lost! Unsaved people are just acting–unsaved! If we truly want to see the social order redeemed and morality restored, we had better get back to seeing *people* redeemed and restored.

But there may be something far more sinister at work here. Perhaps *our* hearts need to be changed every bit as much as the hearts of the unsaved. Evangelicals are not perceived by others to be compassionate people. In the eyes of most unbelievers we seem like Jonah–not really *wanting* the unrighteous to find forgiveness. We seem to enjoy thundering God's judgment; the prospect that drug lords, terrorists and sexual deviants might actually repent and find forgiveness sends us into a psychological tailspin, just as it did Jonah. In fact, the prophet was so "depressed" over God's kindness that he wanted God to take his life![3]

After Jonah had trumpeted his prophetic warning to debauched Nineveh, the city came clean before God with heartfelt repentance. But was Jonah pleased that God's mercy had overridden His judgment? Hardly! "I *knew* that You are a gracious and compassionate God," Jonah whined. "I *knew* You would be slow to anger and abounding in mercy toward this ungodly city. I *knew* You would relent from sending calamity on these Ninevites. Just what kind of God *are* You anyway?" (See Jonah 4:2.)

Good question. Here's a small part of the answer. Unlike the Hindu gods, He is perfect, and one omnipotent God suffices for every human cry for divine intervention. Unlike the Islamic concept of Allah, God goes far beyond mere mercy to bestow free grace and family status to undeserving sinners. Unlike the concept even some Christians have of God, because of the cross God's first disposition toward humanity is *love*, not *judgment*. Christ's sacrifice ratified the end of hostilities between God and humanity. And lest we forget, it is because God *is* "gracious and compassionate . . . slow to anger and abounding in love" that *we* ever got into His family![4]

If we truly want to see the social order redeemed and morality restored, we had better get back to seeing *people* redeemed and restored.

Now, what about you? Whom are you judging? Whom do you write off as past redemption? Look at those whom Christians often despise. What about rage-filled zealots who blow up U.S. marine barracks or bomb our ships? What about African slave traders who treat Christian women as chattel property, or doctors who get rich by terminating pregnancies, or government officials who "neutralize" Christians just for attending an "unregistered" church? What if *they* started repenting and professing faith in Jesus?

Jonah's adamant refusal to carry God's heart left him spiritually and emotionally drained. Eventually he suffered dementia, deeply absorbed in the fate of his shade-giving vine with little interest in the fate of thousands of people in Nineveh. While we might view Jonah's actions as somewhat deranged, his attitude mirrors that of many who are more concerned with their own shade and shelter than the impending doom of the city. A love *of* the world has short-circuited love *for* the world. The Bible warns us, "Stop loving this evil world and all that it offers you, for when you love the world, you show that you do not have the love of the Father in you" (1 John 2:15, NLT). Dietrich Bonhoeffer was right: "Our hearts have room for only one all-embracing devotion, and we can cleave to only one Lord."[5]

The "balanced life" being taught in many circles today has produced people who are passionate all right—passionate about all the wrong things! I saw a magazine ad recently with the headline, "Pity the person who isn't passionate about his furniture." Dear God, what have we become? Teenagers who live for the next party, singles whose driving ambition is "washboard abs," men who are still buying toys at fifty—surely God had more in mind for us than this! One leader observed, "To care for the numbers of poorly converted, weak and self-absorbed converts we have produced in the charismatic movement, we have created a vast life-support system that diverts our time and talent from God's priorities."[6]

Isn't it time to be done with "lesser things" and embrace God's priorities? Will you trade in "the American dream" for God's dream? Ralph Winter, founder of the U.S. Center for World Missions, issues this challenge: "Will you face the rupture of personal priorities the timetable of history will inevitably impose upon all who take [the missions mandate] seriously? Can you 'drink the cup' of the ordeal of finally, definitely exchanging your American passion for a new career, to a much more freeing passion to believe and obey within a cause?"[7] There is indeed a Christ to live for, and there is a cause worth dying for.

PASSION, COMPASSION AND CO-PASSION

Winston Churchill defined a *fanatic* as "someone who can't change his mind and won't change the subject."[8] I am fanatically committed to the sure hope that Jesus will be known, loved and worshiped by all peoples. I cannot change my mind because my mind is bound by Scripture. I will not change the subject because my heart is conquered by Him. By this definition, may God give us more fanatical churches and fanatical Christians.

A love *of* the world has short-circuited love *for* the world.

Any church that is not seriously involved in world evangelization has forfeited its biblical right to exist! Any Christian who just flat does not care whether or not people crash into eternity without God does violence to the heart of the gospel and the heart of Jesus. Such a Christian is a walking paradox, no matter how orthodox his or her theology may be.

When you leave the plains of mediocrity known as "the balanced life," you begin to scale the heights and breathe the rarified air that invigorates faith, hope and love. Love is the mainspring of all effective ministry and the source from which all missions passion flows. God is ready and willing to give you a fresh baptism of compassion. He wants to perform "eye surgery" so you can see once again with clarity, sharpness and focus. Are you willing for this surgery?

If you are willing, I challenge you to pray two dangerous prayers. I promise you in advance that God will answer these prayers. And here's a caveat: If you sincerely pray these simple prayers, you will be saying farewell to the balanced life.

Farewell to the Balanced Life

First, *ask the Holy Spirit to pour God's love into your heart.* The Bible says, "The love of God has been poured out in our hearts by the Holy Spirit who was given to us" (Rom. 5:5). This *agape* love is the fruit of the Spirit (Gal. 5:22–23). Let God remove the anger, bitterness and indifference and transplant His love.

Those with the missions addiction not only *live* dangerously—they *love* dangerously. They dare to love outcasts, society's rejects and even those who violently oppose them. But even more than their love for the lost, they nurture their love for God and their passion for His glory to drench the earth. They can say along with missionary Henry Martyn, "With Thee, O my God, is no disappointment. I shall never have to regret that I have loved Thee too well."

Second, *ask God for the gift of tears.* "Those who sow in tears shall reap in joy. He who continually goes forth weeping, bearing seed for sowing, shall doubtless come again with rejoicing, bringing his sheaves with him" (Ps. 126:5–6). God has entrusted us with the precious, life-producing seed of the gospel. When that seed is watered with tears, it produces a bumper crop.

I am not suggesting that we become emotional basket cases. But perhaps the truly imbalanced are not the sensitive but the insensitive. No doubt the religious leaders of Jesus' day were "balanced" men. They led rote worship and quoted prophetic Scripture with aplomb, devoid of any emotion. By contrast, those who get emotional when it comes to God's glory and peoples' needs are in good company. Unlike His religious contemporaries, Jesus was consumed with a holy jealousy for God's glory. As the perfect God-man He gave the proper emotional response in every situation. At the grave of a friend "Jesus wept" (John 11:35). In worship He "rejoiced in the Spirit" (Luke 10:21). He often punctuated His praying "with loud cries and tears" (Heb. 5:7, NIV).

When conditions warrant it, we ought to weep. Daily I

pray that I will not go through these decisive first years of the new millennium in some kind of spiritual stupor, drugged by entertainment or indifference and unresponsive to the world's agonies. Is it "normal" to be so emotionally "balanced" in a world like ours? This brave new world of the twenty-first century demands that we raise the bar, rediscover the biblical norm and redefine "normal" Christian behavior. Years ago, Watchman Nee challenged believers to live the "normal Christian life." But the *normal* is not the *usual*. Nee observed that "we have seen the subnormal for so long that when we see the normal we think it's abnormal."

Isn't it time to be done with "lesser things" and embrace God's priorities?

The normal Christian life is anything but balanced, as popularly defined. The normal Christian life made Paul and Silas sing in prison and led faith-filled believers to forego deliverance for a better resurrection. If we are "new nature normal," we love our enemies and pray for those who use us. Normal Christians quickly forgive those who wrong them. They wake up in the middle of the night heartbroken for people groups whose names they can barely pronounce. The normal Christian life is high risk and high joy. The normal Christian life releases the temporal to embrace the eternal. It is a life lived in the love of God.

It is normal for us to be passionate about what God is passionate about! Mike Downey, founder and president of Global Missions Fellowship, has observed, "What money is to a banker, passion is to a Great Commission Christian." It is the tender with which we transact kingdom business. God is passionately committed to the worship of His Son by every people, so we should be passionately committed to the worship of His Son by every people. This is not a call to discard balance but rather to redefine it. Yes, there is a rhythm to life, and long-term effectiveness mandates that, like our Lord, we have seasons when we "come aside . . . and rest a while" (Mark 6:31). It's OK to stop and smell the roses. But the flip side of that coin is that there is also a time to "spend and be spent" for the gospel.

God is not calling us to win the world and, in the process, lose our families. But I have known those who so enshrined family life and were so protective of "quality time" that the children never saw in their parents the kind of consuming love that made their parents' faith attractive to them. Some have lost their children, not because they weren't at their soccer games or didn't take family vacations, but because they never transmitted a loyalty to Jesus that went deep enough to interrupt personal preferences.

I happen to be married to the most wonderful woman in the world (and that is not poetic license!). We have been married for almost thirty years, and both of our grown sons are committed followers of Jesus Christ. While I was careful to arrange my schedule to be home on all the important days, our sons were raised with me gone much of the time in ministry around the world. Now that they are grown, I have asked our sons if they carry any resentment for my protracted absences. Both of them assure me that they don't. Why? Because when I was away, Naomi would tell our boys, "Isn't it wonderful that we can share your dad with so many people in the world who need Jesus?"

If we truly believe people are eternally lost without Christ, we can never emotionally "clock out" at the end of a forty-hour workweek. We continue in sync with His heart, and that produces an urgency in all we do. Jesus said, "I must work the works of Him who sent Me while it is day; the night is coming when no one can work" (John 9:4).

Before you read this next paragraph, ask the Holy Spirit to prepare your heart.

While in my study one Sunday afternoon preparing to speak on the vastness of world harvest, I was suddenly overwhelmed by the sheer numbers of unsaved human beings. Quickly calculating a total of 5.384 billion inhabitants on earth [there are now well over 6 billion], with only 1.5 billion of them even professing Christianity, I arrived at a minimum of 3.884 billion individuals alive on planet earth today who are on their way to an eternity without God. Allowing one foot per person in a single file line and compressing the line so tightly that not even a piece of paper could fit between the individuals, I pictured the line beginning in front of the pulpit of our sanctuary in Baton Rouge, Louisiana. To my amazement, my calculations showed it stretched east to the coast of Georgia and over the entire Atlantic Ocean. Crossing Europe, spanning all of Russia and China, it even bridged the vast Pacific and touched California before reentering our church sanctuary in the western entrance. It made an entire revolution around the earth! My heart raced faster with discovery. I continued my calculation to discover the line circling the globe twice . . . four times . . . eight times. I was almost in tears with compassion as I continued circling the globe with line after line of the eternally lost . . . twenty-five lines around.[9]

I read those lines to a friend one day as we sat in my car. As I read, tears glistened in his eyes. By the time I was finished, he was sobbing, pouring out his heart to God on behalf of the billions in our world in need of Jesus Christ. Is it any wonder that this friend is also one of the best witnesses

This brave new world of the twenty-first century demands that we raise the bar, rediscover the biblical norm and redefine "normal" Christian behavior.

for Christ I know? Are you surprised to know that he heads a worldwide missions organization that sees thousands come to Christ each year and has been responsible for planting hundreds of new churches?

IN SYNC WITH GOD

Theologian Emil Brunner observed, "The church exists by mission as fire exists by burning." Yet many in the church seem clueless to God's purposes for them or for their world. They are choking on trivia, drowning in minutia.

Contrast this with a conversation I had with a young man who had recently come to Christ out of the surfing scene in southern California. He told me, "David, I didn't grow up in church. My family never went to church, even on Easter or Christmas. I never attended a Sunday school class, and before I was saved I never heard a sermon except for a few sentences as I surfed the channels on television. But since I received Christ I've been reading the Bible ferociously. I'm growing, and there are a lot of things I still don't understand.

But it didn't take me long to realize that Jesus left His church a job to do."

Here is a young man with no Christian upbringing whatsoever. Yet with his first orientation to Christianity he implicitly understands that Jesus has given a great assignment—a Great Commission—to His followers. How is it that so many who have been in church for decades still haven't figured that out? God put you here on purpose—His purpose. When you were born again, He did not merely give you a fire insurance policy to keep you out of hell.

The Bible is very clear about why Christ redeemed us: "Christ has redeemed us from the curse of the law...that the blessing of Abraham might come upon the Gentiles in Christ

God put you here on purpose— His purpose. Get in hot pursuit of the reason why Jesus took hold of you.

Jesus" (Gal. 3:13–14). Take a look at that again. Paul is answering one of the key questions of Christianity: *Why did God save us?* Here's the astounding answer: Christ redeemed us *in order that* the blessing of Abraham—the blessings we enjoy by being in covenant with the one true God—might come on the nations through Christ. Part of your "redemption package" is an assignment to bring the blessings of salvation to the nations. The word translated "Gentiles" is the Greek word *ethne*, literally the people groups clustered by a common ethnicity, culture and language.

As the seed of Abraham through faith in Christ, we are blessed to be a blessing to all the families of the earth (Gen. 12:1–3). In covenant with God, we are blessed with every spiritual blessing in Christ (Eph. 1:3). This begins a cycle of blessing. We are blessed to be a blessing, not only to those in the natural traffic patterns of our lives, but we are to extend covenant blessings through the gospel to all the families *(ethne)* of the earth. This is the corporate assignment of God's people. That is why there is no such thing as a non-evangelistic Christianity. At the very core of the covenant is God's passionate commitment to bless all the peoples of the earth that they, in turn, might bless Him. Therefore, any church that is not involved in bringing covenant blessing to the nations has forfeited its biblical right to exist.

Within the church's corporate assignment to bless all peoples with the gospel you also have a personal assignment that helps fulfill the corporate assignment. There is a specific something God wants your life to accomplish for His glory in your generation, and only you can do it.

Are you pressing in to discover that unique "something" that only your life can accomplish? Paul said, "I press on, that I may lay hold of that for which Christ Jesus has also laid hold of me" (Phil. 3:12). In effect he was saying, "Just as tenaciously as Jesus took hold of me, I am going to passionately pursue the unique reason why He brought me to Himself." Get in hot pursuit of the reason why Jesus took hold of you. Pursue *that* and fulfill *that* for His glory. In the process, you will find deep personal fulfillment.

God is passionately committed to the global honor of His Son. When our hearts are aligned with His, this becomes our passionate commitment, too. I recently saw an amazing illustration of this on a television program. Two human hearts had literally been extracted from the chest cavities of their donors. One heart was stronger than the other, but the rhythm of each heart was beating independently. Something amazing happened, however, when the two hearts were joined. When one heart was tied to the other, the weaker heart adopted the rhythm of the stronger heart. The rhythms came into perfect sync. This is what happens when we tie our heart to God's heart. We stop marching to our own drumbeat. We stop listening to our own life rhythms. Instead, we step in cadence with the heartbeat and rhythm of God.

God is scanning the earth right now looking for those whose hearts beat with His. "For the eyes of the LORD run to and fro throughout the whole earth, to show Himself strong on behalf of those whose heart is loyal to Him" (2 Chron. 16:9).

Those with the missions addiction experience a divine progression. First, we experience *passion* to see the Great Commission fulfilled. This inevitably leads to *compassion* for the billions without God and thus without hope. Then we experience what Steve Hawthorne calls *co-passion,* where God's passion becomes our passion. The Father is passionately committed to the global honor of His Son, and we "co-passionately" commit to the Father's purpose. The Son is passionately committed to the global honor of His Father, and we "co-passionately" commit to the desire of God's Son. These deep yearnings become a "threefold cord" that binds us to the missions addiction. Great Commission passion is fed by God's compassion, and vice versa. A heart of compassion leads to "co-passion" with Him to see His glory revealed to all peoples.

WHERE THE FIRE ALWAYS BURNS

I received Jesus Christ into my life as a little boy in Vacation Bible School on June 12, 1953. I still remember scenes from that day. I remember what appeared to be hundreds of children, singing songs to Jesus, including this one:

Into my heart, into my heart,
Come into my heart, Lord Jesus.
Come in today; come in to stay.
Come into my heart, Lord Jesus.

Farewell to the Balanced Life

I recall Mrs. Gertrude Nathan, looking like the quintessential VBS teacher in her wire-rim glasses and cotton print dress, telling the old, old story. Then I recall kneeling at an old-time altar at the front, and praying that simple, eternity-altering prayer with words similar to these:

Lord Jesus, thank You for dying on the cross
for me. Right now I turn away from all my sins.
Come into my heart, Lord Jesus. Take my sins
away. I want to be Your child from now on.
Help me to live for You all the days of my life.

That was almost fifty years ago. Just a few years ago I was back at that very church where I had first opened my heart to Christ. I walked into the auditorium in the afternoon when no one was there. It looked much the same as it did in 1953. I walked to the front and knelt again at the altar, at the very place where decades earlier my life had been eternally redirected. I just knelt and worshiped, thanking God again for so great salvation. Soon hot tears were coursing down my face. There, at the altar, I made a fresh commitment to spend the rest of my life getting what happened to me there . . . to others.

If it's not a physical place, I pray there is a place in your heart where you go back and let gratitude grip your heart again, a personal altar where you offer your life to Him in awestruck worship. You see, I know a place where the fire always burns. The Lord said, "A fire shall always be burning on the altar; it shall never go out" (Lev. 6:13). The altar is a place of consecration and renewed devotion. Heaven's mission requires heaven's fire. Ministry is not just the discovery of our spiritual gifts; it is propelling those gifts with heaven's fire. That's why Paul urged Timothy to "fan into flame the gift of God, which is in you" (2 Tim. 1:6, NIV).

You can build an altar anywhere. Finney's altar was a law office where God's love so overwhelmed him he thought he might die of sheer joy. Moody's altar was a crowded New York street where he was sovereignly baptized in the Holy Spirit. Cassie Bernall's altar of sacrifice was a high school classroom.

Amy Carmichael served Christ for fifty years in India without a furlough. Her passion for God's glory and her anger against the devil's treachery led her to courageously expose Hinduism's "dirty little secret" and rescue dozens of children from temple prostitution. One day she penned these words at her own heart-altar:

Give me the love that leads the way,
The faith that nothing can dismay,
The hope no disappointments tire,
The passion that will burn like fire.
Let me not sink to be a clod;
Make me Thy fuel, Flame of God.[10]

What about you? Have you built an altar and placed on it the sacrifice of your "balanced life"? If you will build the altar, God will bring the fire.

If you will build the altar, God will bring the fire.

When I was in college, a missionary recruitment poster showed a picture of Jim Elliot navigating a jungle river. The words on the poster struck me like a club to my stomach:

Jim Elliot
1927–1956
Honor student
All-star athlete
Martyred missionary
Poor Jim. He could have been a success.

Farewell to the Balanced Life

Long before Jim Elliot laid down his life in the jungles of Ecuador, he built an altar of consecration in his dorm room one night at Wheaton College. On that altar he offered the carcasses of "success" and a "balanced life." Journaling what he felt that night in 1948, he wrote:

God, I pray Thee, light these idle sticks of my life and may I burn for Thee. Consume my life, my God, for it is Thine. I seek not a long life, but a full one, like You, Lord Jesus.[11]

Elliot's passionate, prophetic prayer was answered. Only that kind of offering will bring His glory to every tribe and every person. May you find the altar, and the fire.

A man may go aside today, and shut his door, and as really spend an hour in India for God . . . as though he were there in person.
—S. D. GORDON

Every person ought to pray at least one violent prayer every day.
—GORDON LINDSAY

Prayer is essentially a partnership of the redeemed child of God working hand in hand with God toward the realization of His redemptive purposes on earth.
—JACK HAYFORD

FIVE

Triple Threat in the Heavenlies

All nations whom You have made shall come and worship before You, O Lord, and shall glorify Your name.
—PSALM 86:9

Ask of Me, and I will give You the nations for Your inheritance, and the ends of the earth for Your possession.
—PSALM 2:8

We have come for you to tell us."

These were the words of a Quiche leader to Mark Geppart. Here is Mark's amazing story:

High in the mountains of Guatemala is a small Indian village called Zaqualpa. Several years ago my wife and I were working with a group of missionaries attempting to reach the Quiche people of the region. We flew up to the village in a single-engine plane to spend

89

time at a very small mission station there.

My wife and I are both of German extraction, so our eldest son's hair was that white silky blonde that adorns the heads of European children. He was just learning to walk at the time. On the mission field, because of the risk of parasites we carried him in a backpack frame, rather than letting him crawl about in the dust.

The day was fraught with a string of interruptions and much last-minute packing. Finally we took off; when we arrived at the village it was nearly dusk. The pilot buzzed the dirt strip to chase off grazing cows and playing kids. Then, with a tight "hammerhead"-type turn we reversed direction and landed out of a huge red sun. Heads spinning, but laughing with relief and joy, we tumbled from the plane and quickly unloaded our gear so the pilot could get back to the city before dark.

I hoisted Sam into his carrier on my back and walked the thirty meters or so to the three-by-four-meter wooden shed that would be our home for the next few days. Ellie brought armloads of "stuff" for the mission station there, and we were pleasantly greeted by Audrey who lived there.

Getting settled was fun. We had things for Audrey and shared the news of the city and around the globe. She was a wonderful grandmother who was ministering the love of Jesus in those remote mountain villages.

Our socializing was interrupted by the sound of many people outside the building. It sounded as if the place was surrounded and a guerilla war going on in the region. We became quite concerned.

I was chosen to answer the knock at the door. As it swung open we could see hundreds of Quiche people. They were dressed in their beautifully colored earth tones of woven wool. Their jet black hair was braided with beautiful streaming ribbons.

The men were quite small, but appeared very strong. The leader addressed me first in a dialect I did not understand, and then in Spanish.

"We have come for you to tell us," he said in a clear, dignified voice.

"To tell you what?" I asked, without the faintest idea of what he meant.

"The way to God. Our legend tells us that at the time of the red sun a man will come from the sky carrying a child with golden hair, and he will tell us the way to God. You have come from the red sun, and there is the child with golden hair, and we have all come to hear of the way to God."[1]

This story reminds us again of God's passionate intent to be known by all peoples. And when all the secrets are revealed, we will discover that someone somewhere was praying for God's revelation to come to the Quiche.

In the decade just past, the body of Christ has taken enormous strides in our understanding of prayer, spiritual warfare and worship. These three "aboveground" interactions—*global intercession, spiritual warfare* and *prophetic worship*—are playing a major role in the church's missions advance. Together, they represent what I call a "triple threat in the heavenlies."

ASK OF ME

I refer to these activities of the spirit as a "threat" because of their potential to reconstruct the spiritual landscape, turning the futures of entire peoples "from darkness to light, and from the power of Satan to God, that they may receive forgiveness of sins" (Acts 26:18). Missions in this decade is building on thirty years of a remarkable move of God's Spirit. The seventies witnessed the Jesus Movement and the proliferation of the charismatic movement. The eighties were

Global intercession, spiritual warfare and prophetic worship are playing a major role in the church's missions advance.

marked by power evangelism, and the nineties by intercession on a scale never previously seen. We are entering a decade that has been preceded by more signs and wonders and more prayer than in any other thirty-year span in history.

We could well be entering world missions' "due season." The Bible says that Christ "gave Himself a ransom for all, to be testified in due time" (1 Tim. 2:5–6). As Steven Hawthorne and Graham Kendrick point out, "Paul knew that God had appointed his day as a critical juncture for the advance of the Word of God throughout the world . . . But Paul knew that he couldn't do it alone. God's appointment of the time and His assignment of missionaries wasn't enough to assure that God's people would fully meet the moment. What was needed? Paul knew that the moment in history required the most comprehensive prayer effort ever called for in biblical history."[2] That's why Paul pleads with the church: "I desire therefore that the men pray everywhere, lifting up holy hands, without wrath and doubting" (1 Tim. 2:8).

Hawthorne and Kendrick continue: "Many believe that God is appointing this present hour as a unique *kairos* hour of opportunity for the completion of world evangelization. If we follow Paul's line of thought, we'll recognize that opportune times and assigned missionaries won't be enough. To meet the moment, it's going to require every family within God's people to pray for every person in every place."[3]

More prayer is needed at this juncture than ever. It's time to bring closure on the Great Commission, and that will require a massive prayer surge. As has often been said, "The fate of the world is in the hands of nameless saints." In Ezekiel 36 there is an astounding parallel story of cause and effect. There is a vivid acting out of the interaction between God's sovereign intent and man's intercession. God had just given spectacular promises of restoration to Israel. Then, as if to put His seal of assurance on these promises, He reiterates, "I, the LORD, have spoken it, and I will do it" (Ezek. 36:36). When God backs up His promises like that, you can go to the bank on it.

But in the very next verse—after assuring His people that these promises were a "done deal"—God still says they must petition Him in order to see these promises fulfilled! "I will also let the house of Israel inquire of Me to do this for them" (v. 37). In the same way, God has given unfailing promises to us that He will get glory from *every* tribe and nation. But it won't happen until the people of God inquire of Him to do this.

Just prior to Jesus' receiving worship from His completed church, comprised of redeemed men and women from every people and nation, a presentation is made to Him. The Lamb of God is presented "golden bowls full of incense, which are the prayers of the saints" (Rev. 5:8). The worship from every tribe does not come to Him—indeed, it *cannot* come to Him—until the bowls of incense, the prayers of the saints, are full. Prayer is the great condition of the Great Commission.

Accelerated prayer for the harvest generates laborers for the harvest. Is there a correlation between the fact that Singapore has the most advanced cooperative prayer strategy of any national church and the fact that the Singaporean church sends more missionaries per capita than any other nation? You'd better believe it.

David Bryant has observed that most major missions movements have involved five phases: 1) movements of prayer, which 2) renew the vision of Christ (Col. 1:27), 3) lead to unity and resolve in the church to get on with the work of Christ together, 4) revitalize current ministries and 5) expand the work of the kingdom where Christ has not been known before among the unreached.[4]

Our vision of Christ is renewed by personal, daily time with Him. The prime mover of the Student Volunteer Movement in the early twentieth century was a visionary missionary statesman named John R. Mott. Mott sustained a vigorous schedule well into his eighties by a daily practice of extended prayer first thing in the morning. His motto was, "With God everywhere. Without Him, not over the threshold."

Prayer not only renews us, it can remake nations. Think of the silent pleas of millions of Christians throughout the Cold War for the breaking open of the Iron Curtain to the gospel. Then suddenly—*suddenly*—it happened. Anne Graham Lotz notes, "There was no logical explanation for this dramatic series of events except that 'the bowls full of incense, which are the prayers of the saints,' had filled up! I wonder whose prayer was the last one to come in before God said, 'I have all I need in order to proceed to accomplish my purpose.'"[5]

One of the most catalytic persons calling the church to "pray to the Lord of the harvest" is Peter Wagner. In a recent article, Dr. Wagner noted ten major prayer innovations and ten major prayer milestones of the past decade.[6] Among the prayer innovations, he mentions personal intercession for leaders and prayerwalking. Wagner continues to call the church to prayer that makes a difference. To empower the prayers of believers for spreading the gospel, he recently called on churches to make an annual "Josiah Declaration"—a spiritual "house cleaning" that follows the Old Testament king's example of rooting out idolatry from among God's people.[7]

Steven Hawthorne has been instrumental in calling

thousands of believers to "pray on site with insight."[8] And just as God called Joshua to walk out his inheritance, thousands of intercessors today are going to the unreached peoples of the earth to pray and believe God for gospel breakthroughs among them.

Some fifty million Christians were involved in the Praying Through the Window initiatives in the nineties. Hundreds of thousands pray systematically for nations using Patrick Johnstone's *Operation World* (a gold mine of missions data).[9] Ed Silvoso has spearheaded prayer evangelism through the Lighthouse Movement, which has transformed thousands of

Prayer not only renews us, it can remake nations.

Christian homes into lighthouses for the evangelization of their neighborhoods. Silvoso describes prayer evangelism as "talking to God about people before you talk to people about God." Drawing on Luke 10:5, 8–9, Silvoso says that prayer evangelism includes 1) speaking peace to them, 2) fellowshiping with them, 3) taking care of their needs and 4) proclaiming the good news.[10]

I am deeply grateful personally for Roger and Charlotte Merschbrock, personal intercessors for the ministry of Global Advance and for Naomi and me. A committed team of intercessors pray for us, but Roger and Charlotte are what Peter Wagner would refer to as "I-1 intercessors." They see it as a calling from God to pray daily for us. Dr. Wagner notes, "Pastors, missionaries and Christian leaders of all kinds are now enjoying much more blessing in their ministries by having personal intercessors doing spiritual warfare on their behalf, as Euodia and Syntyche were doing for Paul and his team."[11]

In Psalm 2:8, the Father entreats the Son, "Ask of Me, and I will give You the nations for Your inheritance." Through the new birth, we are so intertwined with Jesus that the Bible says we are "in Christ." Therefore, from our position in Him, and in His behalf, we can petition the Father that the nations be given to His Son as His inheritance—"the reward of His sacrifice."

Evangelism is not merely the convincing of the mind, it is also the unshackling of the will.

Dr. Wagner often says with rejoicing that "the international prayer movement is out of control!" Thank God, it's true. It is simply too big to quantify. And yet—and yet, there remains a desperate need for more recruits into the international prayer army. I'm calling on you to become a behind-the-scenes world changer through prayer. Your prayers can make a world of difference.

WARFARE AND WARNINGS

The second activity in the "triple threat" is spiritual warfare—combating demons, principalities and spiritual rulers who hold sway over peoples and geographic areas. But before we start sparring with principalities and powers, let's be sure we're seriously interceding before God every day in behalf of nations and unreached peoples. In other words, prayer should always precede warfare.

Evangelism is not merely the convincing of the mind, it is also the unshackling of the will. It is a literal eye surgery on those who have been blinded by Satan. "But even if our gospel is veiled, it is veiled to those who are perishing, whose minds the god of this age has blinded, who do not believe, lest the light of the gospel of the glory of Christ, who is the image of God, should shine on them" (2 Cor. 4:3–4). Often in order for the hearts of people to be open, the designs of the devil must be shut. Peter Wagner comments:

Jesus not only commissioned Paul to evangelize the nations, but He also outlined his job
description. He told Paul that when he entered
a given people group he would find them
under an awesome power, the power of Satan.
His job would be "to open their eyes and to
turn them from darkness to light, and from the
power of Satan to God" (Acts 26:18).

This was no small task. Satan is none other
than "the god of this age" (2 Cor. 4:4), and "the
prince of the power of the air" (Eph. 2:2). The
nations to which Paul was to take the message
were all under the power of Satan, and they
had been for millennia. Satan fully intended to
keep these nations under his dominion, and he
was not willing to let any of them go without a
fight. The fight would consist of what we call
today "spiritual warfare."[12]

It's important to note that the goal of spiritual warfare is the
liberation of people and the establishing of the lordship of
Christ. Robert Stearns reminds us, "When we talk about warfare, the *goal* of our warfare is not the battle, but the lordship
of Christ we seek to bring to every domain . . . He paid for
them with His blood, and He wants them for His own . . . the
people we may be tempted to vilify and demonize are hurting,
broken people who need the love of Jesus."[13]

The *Transformations* videos, produced by George Otis, Jr.
and the Sentinel Group, chronicle how informed intercession and strategic-level spiritual warfare have been used of
the Lord to bring quantifiable change to several geographic
areas. To prepare the soil for abundant spiritual harvest,
believers first did their homework regarding what had historically prevented harvest in that particular area. "The need
for spiritual mapping is rooted in its purpose," Otis observes.

"Large-scale conversions are unlikely to occur unless we discern the nature and origin of obstacles to revival and receive God's prescribed strategies for their removal."[14]

Jesus has given us keys of the kingdom—strategies that release His rule. One of those strategies is to discern the prevailing principality over a people or region and neutralize its authority by wielding the authority of Christ. Wagner writes, "Binding the strongman, in this case Beelzebub, ruler of the demons, is a description of what we call in today's language strategic-level spiritual warfare . . . Time after time in the Book of Acts we will see spiritual warfare in action: in western Cyprus with Bar-Jesus the sorcerer, in Philippi with the Python spirit, in Ephesus with Diana of the Ephesians and others."[15]

Intercession coupled with wise warfare yields abundant harvest. Frank Damazio has seen this firsthand as he and other pastors in Portland, Oregon, have experienced a high degree of unity for the harvest. Damazio sees a "need to establish strategic prayer centers in every city, in every church and then in every Holy-Spirit covered home, which will open up a gate to heaven to break through the thick covering of evil and darkness. (See Genesis 28:15–17; John 1:5; 8:12.) We must recognize and stand against the territorial spirits that lie behind the chronic historical problems in our cities. We do this through intercessory prayer, preaching the cross of Christ and moving in the supernatural with power to deliver people."[16]

There is danger in any rescue operation. Few activities in the life of a Christian are more hazardous than taking on evil principalities and powers for the purpose of liberating people. I am not prepared to say that Christians should not engage in strategic-level spiritual warfare. However, we should listen carefully to the concerns and warnings of those who disagree with this practice. This issue is much too serious to degenerate into theological jousting. This is real war, and there are real casualties.

I've seen too much evidence of the positive effects of

spiritual warfare to discard its importance for world evangelization. Conversely, I've seen too many abuses of spiritual warfare—ranging from amusing to foolish to deadly—not to take seriously the warnings that are now being extended from many sectors of the church.[17]

The Intercession Working Group of the Lausanne Committee for World Evangelization has cautioned that an emphasis on spiritual warfare carries the risk of leading us "to think and operate on pagan world views." Frankly I think

Intercession coupled with wise warfare yields abundant harvest.

that's overstating it, but let's acknowledge that the potential does exist. If our focal attraction shifts from Jesus and our identification with Him to demons and their control, we're in serious trouble theologically and psychologically. George Otis, Jr., a strong proponent of spiritual warfare, also reminds us that "the focal point of our prayers should be God, not the devil. Railing at the enemy is reckless and immature. It is also dangerous."[18]

There are thoughtful missiologists and godly believers on both sides of the spiritual warfare issue. For the sake of the gospel there needs to be a fraternal embrace of what binds us together. A notable critic of spiritual warfare has been John Piper, author of the missions classic *Let the Nations Be Glad!* But for those of us who endorse strategic-level spiritual warfare, we need to affirm where we agree with this major voice for world missions. One does not have to espouse every tenet of Reformed Theology to passionately desire, along with Piper, that God's glory fill the earth. Nor are we obliged to become five-point Calvinists to agree wholeheartedly that our sovereign God is ultimately orchestrating the flow of events and that Scripture is the final authority concerning spiritual warfare and all other matters of theology and missiology.

There are charismatics who are sounding the alarm as well. When someone of the missions caliber and credentials of T. L. Osborn cautions against warfare abuse, we need to take note. So when this veteran missionary evangelist urges us to reassess our understanding and undertaking of spiritual warfare, it is wise for us to listen to his counsel. He points us to the church's historic posture of *Cristus victor*—a glorious Christ who already rules over the darkness. "To *fight the fight of faith* means to identify with Jesus Christ in His triumph over Satan," Osborn contends. "Christian believers need not struggle to conquer an enemy that Christ has already defeated. They must carry their witness with boldness and with courage, believing that Jesus, who triumphed over Satan, is at work in them, and that He is *greater in the believer than Satan is in the world.*"[19]

For over fifty years, Osborn's evangelistic meetings have spotlighted a conquering Christ who demonstrates His love and power in every dimension of life. "We have consistently believed that Christ is with us, that God's Holy Spirit is in us and that evil spirits are subject to us," he notes. "If they do not flee from people when we proclaim the gospel, then we cast them out. But we never say or do anything to indicate that we consider them a force *on par* with the Holy Spirit at work in us."[20]

Just as there are "Monday-morning quarterbacks" who are convinced of their prowess but who never actually get in the game, so there are "Sunday-morning prayer warriors" who think they're making a difference in the heavenlies when they're not. A lot of people dabble in spiritual warfare. They scream at the devil in the safe company of fellow believers, then get the spiritual daylights beaten out of them during the rest of the week.

Still others, including Stan Guthrie, an associate news editor for *Christianity Today*, have issued a caveat concerning spiritual warfare practices. Though cautious, Guthrie has nonetheless shown a courteous spirit regarding this important issue. "The warfare movement has . . . brought untold millions into the larger missions movement." Guthrie notes Praying Through the Window, Marches for Jesus and prayer walks. He adds, "God has certainly used those sincere prayers as they have been directed to him. There are signs of spiritual openness in places formerly closed to the gospel, from the Arab Muslim world to the former Soviet Union, and who is to say how much of the credit does or does not accrue to Wagner and company?"[21]

We also need to remember that, as with military exercises in the natural realm, spiritual warfare can be fought on many fronts with many strategies. Some Christians seem to enjoy thoroughly the opportunity to scream at demons—or anything else, for that matter. These are often troubled individuals who have not dealt with their own internal rage. The arena of spiritual conflict is no place for them.

Concerning the proclivity of many Christians to anger, Ed Silvoso notes: "One of the greatest mistakes made in spiritual warfare literature and in practice has been to overlook the power of walking in peace—a weapon truly capable of removing the devil from our midst. What we have foolishly chosen instead is hand-to-hand combat."[22]

Let's stop being children. Spiritual warfare is a serious undertaking. Only serious believers need apply. Not just at some future date, but at this present moment, Jesus has been enthroned "far above all principality and power and might and dominion, and every name that is named . . . He has put all things under His feet" (Eph. 1:21–22). Note the past perfect tense of the verb: Already the Father has put all things under the feet of His Son.

Not only did Jesus take away our condemnation on the cross, He "disarmed principalities and powers" and "made a public spectacle of them, triumphing over them" (Col. 2:14–15). To truly be effective in spiritual warfare, we need to change our vantage point—we're not fighting *for* victory as much as we're fighting *from* victory. We must recover our identification with an almighty Christ.

PRAISES FROM EVERY NATION

John Piper defines *world missions* as "a declaration of the glories of God among all the unreached peoples, with a view to gathering worshipers who magnify God through the gladness of radically obedient lives."[23] That's a good place to begin our look at the third "threat" in the heavenlies—worship of the one true God. Not only were *you* created to bring pleasure to Jesus, "*all things* were created through Him and for Him" (Col. 1:16, emphasis added). As Jonathan Edwards said, "The end of God creating the world was to prepare a kingdom for His Son." Worship is a "threat" to the devil because it loosens the hold of this world's kingdom and prepares the soil for the planting of the kingdom of God.

One of Eric Liddell's great lines in the classic film *Chariots of Fire* is, "God created me for a purpose—for China. But He also made me fast, and when I run I feel His pleasure." I don't know whether the person who wrote that film script is a believer, but that is exquisite practical theology! Liddell, one of the twentieth century's great missionaries, knew that his life's purpose was to glorify God, which he expressed through obedience to his missionary call, and by living out his purpose by joyfully doing what God had gifted him to do. When we execute whatever we do for His pleasure, we get a taste of heaven on earth. That is true worship.

The church around the world is changing in many ways, retooling for the twenty-first century. Perhaps the greatest strides in the global church are in praise and worship, as God fashions a new generation of worshipers. An incredulous world looks on as this new generation worships with abandon. The root of the word *fanatic* comes from the Latin word *fanuum,* which means "temple." It refers to someone so devoted to their particular deity that they practically lived in the temple all the time. Such people were eventually called fanatics—"temple dwellers." For the Christian, the implication is not that we should always be "in church," incessantly going to meetings. Rather, we should always be in His presence.

Spiritual warfare is a serious undertaking. Only serious believers need apply.

I'm told that one of the hottest courses in Bible colleges and seminaries these days is ethnomusicology, the study of the relationship between music and culture. This heightened interest is understandable, since God is accelerating the pace of His unflinching commitment to receive hyper-praise from every people. And often, such praise finds one of its loveliest expressions through music.

You can almost feel the rhythm pulsating through David's psalms. Look again at his song of praise, as he calls on all peoples everywhere to worship the true God of heaven and earth. And as you read this, *feel* his joy in the Lord:

Sing to the LORD, all the earth;
Proclaim the good news of His salvation from day to day.
Declare His glory among the nations,
His wonders among all peoples.
For the LORD is great and greatly to be praised;
He is also to be feared above all gods.
For all the gods of the peoples are idols,
But the LORD made the heavens.
Honor and majesty are before Him;
Strength and gladness are in His place.
—1 CHRONICLES 16:23–27

David understood that every culture, every people, had a unique gift of worship to give back to God. Every culture has a redemptive purpose. Once evangelized and living under the lordship of Christ, each culture provides a beautiful one-of-a-kind expression of worship.

Further, the Bible says that God "has made from one blood every nation of men to dwell on the face of the earth, and has determined their preappointed times and the boundaries of their dwellings, *so that they should seek the Lord,* in the hope that they might grope for Him and find Him, though He is not far from each one of us" (Acts 17:26–27, emphasis added). Notice that God calls us as humans to see both our unity ("from one blood") and our diversity ("preappointed times and boundaries"). All of this is for the purpose of seeking and finding God.

Sosene Leau, in his excellent book *Called to Honor Him,* reaffirms the beauty of the distinctive worship each culture can give back to God. Leau writes, "Your cultural background, whatever it may be, is God's gift to you. God gave the Native Americans their chant, the gallic cultures their romance, the orientals their vast sense of history. He gave these things and more that we might learn from one another, love one another, understand that we all belong to one race, the human race, and in the learning and loving catch a vision of all that He is in His manifold wonder. For each cultural distinction expresses a unique part of His own vast creative nature, power and versatility."[24]

Around the throne of God, the redeemed worshipers will be the bride of Christ, the church. In Christ, there are no more hostile distinctions that divide cultures; no longer is there Jew and Gentile. A new race has resulted from the new birth: Jesus has created "in Himself one new man from the two" (Eph. 2:15). In that sense, the church is "race-less." We are united as one in Christ. At the same time, however, the beauty of our cultural heritages remains, presented to Christ as a trophy of His grace. In both Revelation 5 and 7, cultural distinctions are still recognizable as the one church—the one new race—worships from every tribe and nation.

DECLARE HIS GLORY!

I'm calling you to give up your small ambitions. *To know Him and to make Him known! To love Him and to make Him loved!* This should be our consuming passion.

It was this drive for God's glory to be revealed among all peoples that thrust the early Christians beyond themselves. "It was for the sake of [His] Name that they went out" (3 John 7, NIV). They ached for the fame of His name among every nation! With the psalmist, their hearts' cry was, "May the peoples praise you, O God; may all the peoples praise you" (Ps. 67:5, NIV).

Every culture has a redemptive purpose.

Those who die without faith in Jesus Christ are eternally lost. Surely that should make us missions activists. But it is not our highest motivation. The needs of humanity are immense and desperate. We should identify with those who suffer and seek to heal the open, festering wounds of our world. Although noble, this humanitarian impulse should not be our highest motivation either. Talk of "discovering our destiny" is often just more thinly veiled egotism. If "fulfilling our purpose" simply means finally figuring out what our gifts are and getting a kick out of using them, we're carnal narcissists, no matter how much we may protest to the contrary. But if "fulfilling our purpose" means throwing all our energies, gifts and influence into extending His glory throughout the earth, then we're getting the point.

What would be a fitting, God-honoring offering of gratitude

for Christ's sacrifice on the cross for us? Paul gives us the astounding answer. He said he had "the priestly duty of proclaiming the gospel of God, so that the [nations] might become an offering acceptable to God, sanctified by the Holy Spirit" (Rom. 15:16, NIV).

In other words, the greatest gift of worship we could ever present to God would be to offer redeemed nations, which His blood has purchased, back to Him! And how does this happen? By proclaiming the gospel to the nations! Paul's core craving—his missions addiction—was to present all nations and peoples back to Jesus as the most magnificent expression of worship possible. He was "a minister of Jesus

We are in the midst of a once-in-a-lifetime, bumper-crop spiritual harvest.

Christ to the Gentiles, ministering the gospel of God" for the expressed purpose of presenting them back to Him—"that the offering of the Gentiles might be acceptable, sanctified by the Holy Spirit" (Rom. 15:16). Redeemed men and women purchased by His blood are presented back to Him as the greatest oblation that could ever be given. That is worship indeed.

With Paul, our highest motivation should be to offer all peoples to God as trophies of His grace that He might receive the worth and honor due only to Him. It's no wonder that the new song of the redeemed from every tribe, language and people peals out with the loud declaration, "Worthy is the Lamb who was slain to receive power and wealth and wisdom and strength and honor and glory and blessing!" (Rev. 5:12).

We are in the midst of a once-in-a-lifetime, bumper-crop spiritual harvest. Now more than ever we need to focus on God's glory among every people, not just on the task of missions. *Our service and love is not first to the harvest, it is to the Lord of the harvest!* We long for His honor throughout all the earth. Charles Wesley expressed it magnificently in his great hymn:

My gracious Master and my God,
Assist me to proclaim,
To spread thro' all the earth abroad,
The honors of Thy name![25]

Dick Eastman calls them "a gentle army of worshiping warriors." It's the ever-growing company of those who worship God *with a view to extending His worship* to every people in every nation. This kind of worship often leads to prophetic praying over the nations. These intercessors pick up the cry of the Spirit and align their prayers with the very intercession of the Spirit. When we truly experience God's glory, we will burn with passion to see His glory extended to the nations! With the psalmist, our hearts will cry out, "Be exalted, O God, above the heavens; let Your glory be above all the earth!" (Ps. 57:11).

One of the best definitions of worship was given many years ago by the English clergyman William Temple. Temple defined *worship* as "the submission of all our nature to God. It is the quickening of the conscience by His holiness; the nourishment of the mind with His truth; the purifying of imagination by His beauty; the opening of the heart to His love; the surrender of will to His purpose—and all of this gathered up in adoration, the most selfless emotion of which our nature is capable."[26]

In worship, our imagination is "purified by His beauty," so that we naturally begin to envision the earth "filled with the knowledge of the glory of the LORD, as the waters cover the sea" (Hab. 2:14). As we worship, something begins to well up within us to speak this out as a prophecy to the nations.

I'm convinced that the *proclamation* of the good news of the gospel is not limited to evangelistic preaching. We also proclaim the good news of the gospel and the enthroning of Christ over the nations as we worship. "The testimony of Jesus is the spirit of prophecy" (Rev. 19:10). This is prophetic worship.

Dutch Sheets writes, "God is calling the church to a new understanding of prophetic action and declaration, functioning as His voice and body upon the earth . . . Some will be told to march on land, claiming it for the kingdom of God. Whatever He says to you, do it. Be bold to declare the Word of the Lord over and into situations. Sprinkle the seed of His Word into the earth and expect a harvest."[27]

Over the last several years there has been a lot of teaching regarding the restoration of the tabernacle of David. Whatever other prophetic implications there may be, this promised restoration combines a rejuvenation of worship and spectacular harvest. "'On that day I will raise up the tabernacle of David, which has fallen down, and repair its damages; I will raise up its ruins, and rebuild it as in the days of old; that they may possess the remnant of Edom, and all the Gentiles who are called by My name,' says the LORD who does this thing. 'Behold, the days are coming,' says the LORD, 'when the plowman shall overtake the reaper'" (Amos 9:11–13).

Note the sequence: Worship is restored, the nations come, and then there is unprecedented harvest. Concerning this restored tabernacle of David, Mike Bickle says, "To me, it means worshiping God—using the Word of God to worship God. And it's the anointing of the Spirit to inspire and energize intercessory prayer for the Great Commission to be fulfilled."[28]

To that end, Bickle is developing International Houses of Prayer that combine prayer *for* the nations with prophetic worship *over* the nations. And all of this—as in any true worship—is centered around the beauty of Jesus. In Haggai 2:7, the prophet refers to Him as the Desire of All Nations. Whether they realize it or not, the longing of broken nations and peoples for the establishing of justice and peace is really a longing for Jesus. He comes to shake the nations so He may be enthroned. In doing so, He promises, "I will fill this temple with glory . . . the glory of this latter temple shall be greater than the former" (vv. 7, 9).

God is prompting these innovative expressions of prayer and worship in order to unveil the Desire of All Nations. "IHOP is really about a new paradigm of God, which I call the beauty realm," Bickle notes. "It's the lovesick God who fascinates us, and because we are fascinated we become abandoned. The outsider is gripped by the theology and the model, but the insiders are in a process of being lost in the beauty realm as they intercede for the fulfillment of the Great Commission."[29]

IT'S ALL ABOUT HIM

Someone has observed that much of modern evangelicalism reads like an IRS 1040 form: It's true, all the data is there, but it doesn't take your breath away.[30]

But now a new longing for intimate worship is surfacing. It is, in fact, a bridal longing as the church, the bride of Christ, seeks the honor of the One she adores. As Steve Fry observes:

> The greatest and most militant force the world has ever seen is that of a wife defending her husband! This emphasis is being nourished through worship, and is one reason why the worship movement is gathering steam. If we would see genuine revival then we must recover that sense of bridal affection for Jesus . . . For it is a holy desperation for Him that kindles the flames of ministry for a lifetime. A holy desperation for Him that keeps the Great Commission from becoming merely the great strategy. A holy desperation for Him, which keeps us centered on the one motive that should guide all our endeavors: to give Him pleasure![31]

Sweet strains of hymns sung in harmony drifted with the breezes through the gentle South Pacific air. Splashes of brilliant color covered the football field as thousands of happy Christians marched toward the platform in their tribal dresses and costumes. It was definitely a "Kodak moment!"

They came singing, waving branches, some with shouts of joy, all of them with thankful hearts. When each group reached the platform, large pouches were opened and poured out on a table as coins from children and larger cash from adults swelled into a mound of money. The churches of Fiji had gathered for their annual festival to bring their missions offerings to God.

As I watched this moving scene from the speaker's platform, I wept. God was being lavishly exalted by beautiful island peoples who only a few generations earlier were far from Him. But thanks to God-honoring missionaries, not only had these thousands of Fijians come to Christ, they were eager to honor Him and share Him with others.

I remembered the dying words of the sacrificial missionary John Hunt: "Oh, let me pray for Fiji. O Lord, save Fiji!" Now my eyes were witnessing to a large degree the fulfillment of this missionary's prayer one hundred years earlier. A surge of gratitude raced through my heart as I witnessed firsthand the transgenerational faithfulness of God. What we pray today can break through the time barrier and reverberate in blessing for generations yet unborn.

As I looked again at the tribal group, beautifully distinct yet all singing in harmony as the Lord's one redeemed people, I realized that it was a small foretaste of a future event on a massive scale, which John saw in the spirit.

We are currently in a once-in-a-lifetime opportunity for world evangelization. The missions addiction is not a fixation with a *task* but a magnificent obsession to see the worldwide worship of a *Person*. I am not writing this book merely to champion a cause, even a cause as noble as world missions. What I *am* urging upon all of us is that we so passionately fall in love with Jesus that what is precious to Him becomes precious to us, and what is priority for Him becomes priority for us.

What we pray today can break through the time barrier and reverberate in blessing for generations yet unborn.

So what's it all about? Why all this praying for the nations? Why all this confrontation with principalities and powers? Why all this prophetic worship?

Because God is passionately committed–"fixated" is not an irreverent description–to see His Son known, loved and worshiped by every tribe, language and nation. When we align our hearts with His, this should be our passionate commitment as well. The missions addiction is nothing other than an all-out obsession with the worldwide fame of His name!

What I am calling in this book a "missions addiction" Floyd McClung calls an "apostolic passion." He defines this overarching life passion as "a deliberate, intentional choice to live for the worship of Jesus in the nations. It has to do with being committed to the point of death to spreading His glory. It's the quality of those who are on fire for Jesus, who dream of the whole earth being covered with the glory of the Lord." Those with apostolic passion are hope-driven dreamers. "Your greatest dream is that His name will be praised in languages never before heard in heaven," McClung says. "Your reward is the look of pure delight you anticipate seeing in His eyes when you lay at His feet the just reward of His sacrifice."[32]

Will you be part of "the gentle army of worshiping warriors"? The whole world is watching.

In Muslim eyes Western secularism, irreligiosity, and hence immorality are worse evils than the Western Christianity that produced them. In the Cold War the West labeled its opponent "godless communism"; in the post-Cold War conflict of civilizations Muslims see their opponent as "the godless West."
—SAMUEL P. HUNTINGTON

There are two things that they have need to possess who go on pilgrimage—courage and an unspotted life. If they have not courage, they can never hold on their way; and if their lives be loose, they will make the very name of the pilgrim stink.
—MR. HOLY-MAN IN JOHN BUNYAN'S
THE PILGRIM'S PROGRESS

Do we so appreciate the marvelous salvation of Jesus Christ that we are our utmost for His highest?
—OSWALD CHAMBERS

SIX

The Whole World Is Watching

If you return, then I will bring you back; you shall stand before Me; if you take out the precious from the vile, you shall be as My mouth.
—Jeremiah 15:19

Arise, shine; for your light has come! And the glory of the Lord is risen upon you. For behold, the darkness shall cover the earth, and deep darkness the people; but the Lord will arise over you, and His glory will be seen upon you. The Gentiles shall come to your light, and kings to the brightness of your rising.
—Isaiah 60:1–3

The whole world's watching! The whole world's watching!"

This was the angry chant of hundreds of protesters outside the Democratic National Convention in 1968 as police clubbed them into silence. Whether viewers agreed with their position or not, the protesters' screams were forever etched in the memories of millions. Their message was, "You will not be allowed to act with impunity. The cameras are rolling. The whole world's watching! You will be called to account!"

And so will we.

As never before, the whole world is watching to see if

113

Christians' lives match their words. Much of the anger against us today is a reaction to our duplicity. Muslims decry our immorality, postmoderns scorn our hypocrisy and communists smirk at our lack of commitment. Marilyn Manson has pulled thousands of teenagers into his warped world. I am told that on his website a person can even "accept Marilyn Manson as your personal savior." What blatant blasphemy. Yet I heard this rock icon say in a recent interview that it is not so much the doctrines of Christianity he hates as it is the hypocrisy of Christians.

But why should they care? Why should unbelievers care whether we live up to our profession? The answer, I believe, is tucked away in the story of Jonah's flight away from his missionary call to Nineveh. While the prophet slept, God judged his disobedience with a violent storm. The sailors cried out to their false gods to save them, but to no avail. Finally, Jonah was shaken awake, and he confessed to the sailors, "I know that this great tempest is because of me" (Jon. 1:12).

Suddenly a group of cursing seamen became holiness preachers—preaching to the backslidden prophet! "Why have you done this?" they confronted Jonah. "For the men knew that he fled from the presence of the LORD" (v. 10). Could it be that even a pagan world somehow knows that the reason for the "tempest" is our disobedience? Do they somehow realize that *our* rebellion is imperiling *them?* Could this not be a big part of the reason for their hostility against us? They make no profession of righteousness, but we do. They have no missions mandate, but we do. And when we run from our assignment, our sin endangers everybody.

So what is the greatest detriment to the evangelization of the world today? Is it a lack of money? Is it deficient personnel? Maybe it is a lack of cooperation. Is it obstinate governments or Islamic resistance? Secularism? Postmodernism? What— more than any other factor—is keeping us from fulfilling the Great Commission?

Our failure cannot be laid at the feet of radical Muslims, belligerent governments or disinterested postmoderns. *The greatest impediment to world evangelization today is our own carnality!*

As never before, the whole world is watching to see if Christians' lives match their words.

For two millennia the church has survived both the wrath of its enemies and the sins of its members. To our shame, in some places Jesus has suffered more from His friends than from His enemies. The sin among us is a far greater problem than the rage against us.

When the heat is turned up, however, the gray area disappears. The gospel seems to thrive in the soil of persecution. The fastest-growing church in the world today is in China, yet the government has harassed, persecuted, imprisoned and sometimes martyred Christians since communism came to power in the early 1950s. When Western missionaries were forced out of the country, there were one million Christians. Today there are probably around ninety million believers.

The story leaked out recently of a teenage girl in China who was imprisoned because she oversaw a network of hundreds of illegal house churches. A friend was finally allowed to see her in prison. The friend whispered to the imprisoned girl, "Be encouraged. There are Christians all over the world praying for the church in China."

The imprisoned teenager's reply takes our breath away. "Please tell them to keep praying," the prisoner said, "but please ask them not to pray that the persecution will ease up! Because when we're persecuted, Jesus' presence is more precious and we grow more."

That kind of theology is foreign to most of us in Western

nations. But we need to listen again to our sister's request. We should certainly pray for our brothers and sisters in China and in other restrictive nations. We should ask the Holy Spirit to open doors for a clear proclamation of the gospel and open hearts to receive it. And even if it goes against our Free World sensitivities, we should ask God to engineer the events in China and every nation to bring the greatest leverage for the glory of His name.

The greatest impediment to world evangelization today is our own carnality!

The Chinese government's policy toward Christians is erratic. Yet in this nation where persecution is common and many people groups remain unreached, there are also more Christians than any other geopolitical nation. The lesson is that persecution often purges and prospers the church.

INTEGRITY SHORTAGE

California's energy problems were first described as a "power shortage." As energy supplies continued to dwindle, the problem became an "energy crisis." In the same way, what began as an integrity shortage in the church is now a full-blown crisis.

This brave new world calls for radical holiness—and that doesn't look anything like what most people envision. C. S. Lewis wrote, "How little people know who think that holiness is dull. When one meets the real thing . . . it is irresistible. If even 10 percent of the world's population had it, would not the whole world be happy and converted before a year's end?"[1] True holiness is light-years removed from self-righteousness.

Some time ago a man wanted to know where I was on the theological spectrum. He asked, "What are you anyway?"

I replied, "I'm a global, liberal, evangelical, charismatic

radical!" That's the new breed of Christian God is fashioning for the twenty-first century.

- We need a *global perspective,* intentionally identifying with God's kingdom and God's people worldwide.

- We need a *liberal heart* (not to be confused with liberal theology or liberal politics), embracing all who need to see God's love lived out.

- We need an *evangelical theology,* firmly holding to Scripture and to "the faith which was once for all delivered to the saints" (Jude 3).

- We need a *charismatic experience,* a baptism in the Holy Spirit that launches us into super-natural living.

- And we need a *radical lifestyle* that separates us from a little life and orbits our interests around God's glory.

We should all be grateful for the new call to integrity in the church today, but perhaps we do not hear enough about the love that must undergird it. Long before Promise Keepers, in the 1950s I was a PK—a preacher's kid! My father pastored a church in Tulsa that gave 50 percent to missions, beginning with the first offering they ever took. Of course, since I was a preacher's kid, some of my friends took it on as their assignment to lure me away from my commitment. I was far from the model PK, but when I was tempted growing up to do something wrong, what stopped me was the thought, *I just can't do this to my parents. I love them too much. I've seen how they love Jesus, how they love me and how they joyfully sacrifice for the gospel. I just can't do this because of how it would hurt them and their reputation.*

Today I trust that my thinking has matured to say, *I just*

can't do this to my Lord. I love Him too much. I've seen how He loves me and how He has sacrificed for me. I just can't do this because of how it would hurt Him and His reputation.

Paul reprimanded legalistic believers in Rome for a problem similar to ours today. While they paid lip service to God's law, they dishonored Him by loose lives. Then as now, legalism had the reverse effect of unholiness instead of the intended holiness. This is because holiness of heart comes not by law but by grace. Quoting from Ezekiel, Paul castigated the loose legalists saying, "The name of God is blasphemed among the Gentiles because of you" (Rom. 2:24). Love for the Lord, not legalism and the law, produces attractive holiness. Tragically in our day too, the name of God is blasphemed among the nations because of sin in our midst.

The whole world is watching, hoping to see a "global, liberal, evangelical, charismatic radicalism" that rejects the lure of sin and refuses to be jaundiced by the world's current condition. The unbelieving wish to see among the believing a "brave new church" of clearheaded worshipers who envision God's glory drenching every people and nation (Isa. 11:9). They long to see love lived out. This is what Robert Coleman calls "the Great Commission lifestyle," loving God supremely and loving our neighbor as ourselves (Matt. 22:37–40). Coleman writes:

Out of this Great Commandment flows the Great Commission. Where such love motivates our labor, the effort cannot be in vain; but when it is not the heartbeat of our work, whatever we do will be wasted energy (1 Cor. 13:1–13). In its larger context, then, everything about our lives turns on love.[2]

Jesus said, "You are the salt of the earth . . . you are the light of the world" (Matt. 5:13–14). As such, He calls you to "let your light so shine before men, that they may see your good works and glorify your Father in heaven" (v. 16).

Everywhere we look people are in desperate need. We are called to be salt and light, but Jesus warns that we are not to

Then as now, legalism had the reverse effect of unholiness instead of the intended holiness. This is because holiness of heart comes not by law but by grace.

lose our saltiness nor are we to let our light grow dim. Sin short-circuits God's power in our lives, dulling the flavor and dimming the light.

ALL LOVES EXCELLING

As the inaugural generation of Christians in the twenty-first century, we are setting the standard for generations to come. Yet sin is more open than ever. Some estimates are that one-third of all Internet websites are pornographic. It is tough to even read a newspaper without being assaulted. Michael Brown observed, "The devil is turning up the heat of sin and pollution in our society and we, like the proverbial frog in slow-boiling water, hardly realize the temperature is rising."[3] So how, in century 21, can we be holy?

KEEP FALLING IN LOVE WITH JESUS.

His white-hot love is holy and pure. The truly impressive Christians to me are not the shooting stars who suddenly blast into prominence and often disappear just as quickly. We are great in the hundred-yard dash, but what people are longing to see are world-class, cross-country Christians, those who stay strong and compassionate year after year, decade after decade.

I had to chuckle when a young person asked me recently,

"How do you make it over the long haul?" (I knew then that I was no longer officially young!) Thinking about his question for a moment, I responded, "You make it over the long haul by making it over the short haul." Each day is an opportunity to love Him more passionately or to subtly move away from Him.

KEEP SHORT ACCOUNTS WITH GOD.

We can trust the Holy Spirit to convict us of any attitude, words or actions that dishonor the Lord. Whenever the Spirit brings these to light, a full, immediate repentance brings restored fellowship. Campus Crusade founder, Bill Bright, has introduced thousands to the biblical discipline he calls "spiritual breathing." Whenever the Holy Spirit convicts us of any sin, we immediately confess that sin and make a full repentance. Dr. Bright likens spiritual breathing to exhaling, releasing any pollutants from our heart. Then we inhale by breathing in God's promised forgiveness. "If we confess our sins, He is faithful and just to forgive us our sins and to cleanse us from all unrighteousness" (1 John 1:9). In this way, we live with no unconfessed sin. We keep short accounts with Him.

MEDITATE ON GOD'S WORD DAILY.

As we soak in the Scriptures, our minds are both washed and renewed (Eph. 4:23; 5:26). There are no road maps for the twenty-first century. No one has been here before. So we must go to a source that transcends times and cultures—we must go back to the Bible. Even though it is a brand-new ball game, the "rule book" remains the same. God's Word is a mooring that steadies us even as the very earth shifts beneath us.

BE FILLED WITH THE HOLY SPIRIT.

That is where new dimensions open to us. We experience the promised power—power to live Christ-honoring lives and power to boldly share that life. "But you shall receive power when the Holy Spirit has come upon you; and you shall be witnesses to Me in Jerusalem, and in all Judea and Samaria, and to the end of the earth" (Acts 1:8). "The key to completing the Great Commission is the energizing power of the Holy Spirit," notes author and missionary statesman Robertson McQuilkin, "but the key to unleashing that power is obedient faith, and I'm not all that confident the

God's Word is a mooring that steadies us even as the very earth shifts beneath us.

American church is connecting with Him on those terms."[4] Let's reconnect! It's in the arena of faith and obedience that we experience the Spirit's power.

There is a literal transformation chamber that, because of Jesus, is immediately available to us any time, anywhere. It is the transformation chamber of His presence. We are changed by the very act of *worship*. "But we all, with unveiled face, beholding as in a mirror the glory of the Lord, are being transformed into the same image from glory to glory, just as by the Spirit of the Lord" (2 Cor. 3:18).

BE ACCOUNTABLE TO OTHERS.

To live in "the beauty of holiness" in our day we need to be accountable to others. A mature accountability partner or small accountability groups are a great help. This is where we allow the hard questions to be asked. I am deeply grateful for my accountability relationship with Mike Downey, president of Global Missions Fellowship. As executives of two missions organizations, we hold each other's feet to the fire and require straight answers to straight questions of obedience.[5]

Let us hear again the call to the kind of worship that God accepts: "Worship the LORD *in the beauty of holiness!*" (Ps. 96:9, emphasis added). In love with Jesus, with no unconfessed sin, filled with His Spirit and accountable to one another—that's "incarnational theology" for today.

An old gospel song says:

Trust and obey,
For there's no other way
To be happy in Jesus
But to trust and obey.[6]

So there it is. Trust His promises, obey His Word and thereby be happy in Jesus! Faith and obedience are the keys that will sustain you, even in the direst circumstances. Samuel Zwemer, known by many as the apostle to Islam, saw two of his little girls die in one week in Bahrain. At first the Muslims refused to give permission to Dr. and Mrs. Zwemer for the girls to be buried there since they said the Christians would "contaminate" the soil. Finally they allowed the burial on the condition that Zwemer would dig the graves himself. Imagine the pain in this missionary father's heart as he dug two little graves, put up headstones and wrote on them the words, "Worthy is the Lamb who was slain to receive riches."[7] Though Zwemer was no stranger to tragedy, his friends said that his most noticeable quality, even in old age, was his irrepressible joy.

Then there was Adoniram Judson, the first American missionary. He too lost family members overseas. He was placed on a death march simply as a punishment for the policies of the British government (with which, of course, he had nothing to do). The severity of the march almost broke his health permanently. Yet after these tragedies Judson wrote, "The prospects are as bright as the promises of God."

Faith and obedience brought prevailing joy. Winkie Pratney is right: "God is after two things for your life—that you be happy and holy. And He knows you cannot be really happy until you are holy."[8]

ALL THE WRONG SCANDALS

A happy, holy life will not free us from scandals—it will simply ensure that we are involved with the right ones!

In love with Jesus, with no unconfessed sin, filled with His Spirit and accountable to one another—that's "incarnational theology" for today.

For too long, Christians have been involved in all the wrong scandals. A rehashed antinomianism among us is inferring that "every man can do what seems right in his own eyes." (See Judges 17:6.)[9] Some are even bolder in their deception, placing responsibility for their actions on God. "God told me I should divorce my wife." "God said I can give myself a $100,000 bonus." "God said I don't need to answer to anybody but Him."

Oh, *really?!*

There is the scandalous tragedy of a tidal wave of failed marriages. Did you know that the rate of divorce among evangelicals in America is higher than the average of the population at large?[10] Even more tragic is the literal epidemic of adultery and divorce among Christian leaders. Jack Hayford calls us back to Scripture and back to our marriage vows. "Confused and biblically unfocused thinking is at the center of this crisis and has amplified its impact," writes Hayford. Then this senior statesman warns, "If sound, scriptural administration of the issues surrounding the church, its leaders and their marriages is not soon arrived at with solidarity, there is reason to prophesy widespread deception on other issues as well."[11] This is not to heap guilt on anyone who tried to save his or her marriage and failed. Nevertheless, we must sound the alarm, and we must stop letting our leaders get a "bye" when they flippantly switch life partners and just go on preaching as though it's no big deal. It is a big deal—the whole world is watching.

There are other tragic scandals for which our generation of Christians is famous—or infamous. The misappropriation of huge sums of money has choked the giving impulse of many Christians who have gone from being brokenhearted to being just plain angry. The heavy leveraging of position by some leaders has led to warnings against "toxic" abuses of power.

"Who knows how much God would do for His servants if He dared."

In a day when we need more money than ever to advance missions, scandals of finance have stunted our fiscal strength. And in a day when biblical leadership is in drastically short supply, people are skeptical of visionaries because of past abuses.

I was privileged to be one of over ten thousand evangelists and church leaders from more than two hundred nations who convened for Amsterdam 2000. Flowing from that historic gathering, The Amsterdam Declaration was drafted as a charter for evangelism in the twenty-first century. The Declaration speaks pointedly to the need for Christ-honoring leadership in the church:

The servant of God must adorn the gospel
through a holy life. But in recent times God's
name has been greatly dishonored and the gospel
discredited because of unholy living by Christians
in leadership roles ... We pledge ourselves to be

124

**accountable to the community of faith for our
lives, doctrine, and ministry and to flee from sin,
and to walk in holiness and humility.**

Holiness and humility . . . they go hand-in-hand. Much of the brash assertiveness and rampant arrogance is masking deep insecurities. Yet when we truly understand our dignity in Christ, like Him we can voluntarily take the role of a servant. While accountability is important, it is not our best protection against evil. Our surest defense is to cultivate humility. Andrew Murray counsels, "Believe humility to indeed be the mother-virtue, your very first duty before God, and the one perpetual safeguard of the soul."[12] Did you see that? Andrew Murray believed humility to be the mother-virtue, the cultivated posture of heart from which all other virtues are born.

We have gotten exactly what we have emphasized. We have been strong on faith and soft on sin. As a result, we have produced visionary heavyweights and character bantamweights. Paul Billheimer lamented, "Who knows how much God would do for His servants if He dared."[13] Can people dare to trust us? More importantly, can God dare to trust us? The whole world is watching.

There is one scandal, however, from which we must never hide—the scandal of Christ and the cross! This is the *right* scandal. If we are going to be "nailed" as scandalous, this is where we must take the nails. Jesus Christ is a "stone of stumbling" and a "rock of offense"; the cross and the person of Christ literally trip people up. But this Rock has also become the "chief cornerstone," the very foundation stone of our faith (1 Pet. 2:7–8).

Paul Billheimer wrote:

**To locate the center of history one must
bypass all these vast empires and the glittering
names associated with them and find his way**

to a tiny land called the navel of the earth, the
geographical center of the world. And in that
tiny land is a tiny hill called Calvary, where
two thousand years ago a Man named Jesus
was lifted up to die. And this writer submits
that that tiny hill in that tiny land is the center
of all history, not only of this world, but of all
the countless galaxies and island universes of
outer space from eternity to eternity.[14]

Indeed, "the cross is the center of time and eternity, the
answer to the enigmas of both."[15]

The offense of the cross is that it is a scandalous line of
demarcation, cleaving all humanity into disciples or oppo-
nents. Jesus is opposed—often violently opposed—by those
He and His cross offend. But it is our honor, never our
shame, to stand with Him:

Let us, then, go to him outside the camp, bearing the disgrace he bore. For here we do not
have an enduring city, but we are looking for the
city that is to come. Through Jesus, therefore, let
us continually offer to God a sacrifice of praise—
the fruit of lips that confess his name.
—HEBREWS 13:13–15, NIV

Notice the profound difference: Unrighteous scandals
bring shame; this scandal delivers from shame!

Behold, I lay in Zion a stumbling stone and
rock of offense [*skandalon* in Greek], and whoever believes on Him will not be put to shame.
—ROMANS 9:33

WHAT KIND OF PEOPLE?

In light of the impending Day of the Lord, Peter asks, "What
kind of people ought you to be?" He answers, "You ought to

live holy and godly lives as you look forward to the day of God and speed its coming" (2 Pet. 3:11–12, NIV).

HOLY PEOPLE

In times like these, we should first be *holy people*. "You ought to live holy and godly lives . . . " (v. 11, NIV). Is that the kind of people we are, *really?* The media's perception of evangelical Christians is that we are self-righteous, intolerant and hypocritical. Too often the caricatures of us by late night comedians are too close to reality.

We have codified sin, denouncing two or three "public, national evils" while giving ourselves all sorts of leeway for secret sins of the flesh. Those "big sins" we rail on are probably not much of a temptation for most Christians, so we find it convenient to oppose them. But easy "no-fault" divorce is epidemic among us. Thousands of men show up at church Sunday morning with a secret weight of guilt for indulging in pornography on the Internet or TV Saturday night. Someone said that the new definition for *hypocrite* is a Christian who complains about all the sex and violence on his VCR. David made a commitment that Christian men today would do well to revisit. "I will walk within my house with a perfect heart. I will set nothing wicked before my eyes" (Ps. 101:2–3). It was only when David broke that resolve that his family and influence began to unravel.

HOPEFUL PEOPLE

Peter also says that we need to be *hopeful people*. We are to be "looking for...the coming of the day of God" (2 Pet. 3:12). Fiction writer Jan Karon was asked why her books about simple faith and well-lived lives consistently show up on the *New York Times* Bestseller List. She answered, "Hope is never out of style." Of all people, Christians should be gushing with hope! Modern philosophies have spawned widespread despair. Since any hope of finding meaning evaporated for them long ago, all that's left is to live for the moment. At some point, sex and stimulants don't even satisfy for the moment, and despair sets in. But as others are sinking in despair, they are amazed that the convulsive waves that are drowning them are buoying us! Bible-based hope

One of the best antidotes to being a worldly Christian is to embrace Christ's cause, live for His honor and become a world Christian.

keeps us afloat in the turbulence. That's when we throw out a lifeline of hope—the bedrock assurance of "the coming of the day of God." Jesus shall reign! He will receive His due praise from every tribe, people and nation!

HARVEST PEOPLE

Finally, Peter says we are to be *harvest people*. Not only are we to look for this apocalyptic day of God, we are actually to speed its coming! In some amazing way, we help hasten the coming of the Lord. God allows us the high dignity of participating in His very timetable by helping to fulfill the Great Commission. Jesus said, "And this gospel of the kingdom will be preached in all the world as a witness to all the nations, and then the end will come" (Matt. 24:14). Clearly, there's a cause and effect. The good news of Christ's rule is proclaimed as a witness to *every* people group, and then the end will come!

Holy people, hopeful people, harvest people—in other words, let's be world Christians.

WORLDLY CHRISTIANS OR WORLD CHRISTIANS?

I have not heard the term for years, but preachers used to

warn against being *worldly Christians,* entangled in the carnal whims of the times. This chapter has been a plea for us to tear loose from the obsessions of our age. Instead of being "worldly" Christians, this is a call to be *world Christians!* One of the best antidotes to being a worldly Christian is to embrace Christ's cause, live for His honor and become a world Christian. In other words, one of the surest ways to be spared the contagion of worldliness is to be injected with the missions addiction!

The term *world Christian* was popularized by the late Herbert J. Kane. In fact, the last book before his death was titled *Wanted: World Christians.*[16] Dr. Kane defines a world Christian as . . .

One who acknowledges the universal fatherhood of and the universal lordship of Christ, one who recognizes the cosmopolitan composition of the Christian church and the prime importance of the Christian mission, and one who recognizes his own personal responsibility for all phases of the Christian world mission. A world Christian will seek to increase his knowledge of world affairs, broaden his views of the church, increase his understanding of the Christian mission, enlarge the people of his prayer life, go abroad if opportunity affords, change his lifestyle, and recognize his personal responsibility for world missions.[17]

In short, a world Christian is someone who has found his or her place in God's big plan.

World Christians live for God's global glory and are constrained by Christ's love. They live beyond themselves. "For the love of Christ compels us, because we judge thus: that if One died for all, then all died; and He died for all, that those who live should live no longer for themselves, but for Him who died for them and rose again" (2 Cor. 5:14–15). World Christians serve Christ by serving others. They realize, as Oswald Chambers said, that an effective Christian worker is "not one who proclaims the gospel merely, but one who becomes broken bread and poured out wine in the hands of Jesus Christ for other lives."[18]

World Christians hear voices, not because they are neurotic but because they are sensitized to dimensions most people ignore. At age twenty-two, Jim Elliot wrote in his diary, "Consider the call from the Throne above, 'Go ye,' and from round about, 'Come over and help us,' and even the call from the damned souls below, 'Send Lazarus to my brothers, that they come not to this place.' Impelled, then, by these voices, I dare not stay home while Quichuas perish."[19] God give us a new generation that is "impelled by these voices."

J. Wilbur Chapman was a noted American evangelist of the early 1900s. When he was in London, Chapman met with General William Booth, founder of The Salvation Army. Booth was past eighty years of age when they met. Dr. Chapman listened intently as the old general spoke of his trials, conflicts and victories.

"I will tell you the secret. God has had all there was of me."

The American preacher then asked General Booth if he would disclose his secret of success. "General Booth, how did all this happen? How does one man in one lifetime set so much in motion for the kingdom of God?" Chapman recounted Booth's answer:

He hesitated for a second . . . and I saw the tears come into his eyes and steal down his cheeks, and then he said, "I will tell you the secret. God has had all there was of me. There

130

have been men with greater brains than I, men with greater opportunities; but from the day I got the poor of the world on my heart, and a vision of what Jesus Christ could do with the poor, I made up my mind that God would have all of William Booth there was. And if there is anything of power in The Salvation Army today, it is because God has had *all the adoration of my heart, all the power of my will, and all the influence of my life.*"[20]

Will you lay before Him . . .

■ All the adoration of your heart?

■ All the power of your will?

■ All the influence of your life?

The whole world is watching.

The time for big-thinking, big-hearted American leadership is not over. The national government may be confused about its foreign policy, but the American church is not. We have been clearly commanded by our King to go into all the world, preach the gospel and disciple the nations.
—JOHN DAWSON

The church is God's instrument to communicate the message of Christ to the people of the world, and the local church is His primary instrument.
—LARRY REESOR

We are witnessing the greatest change in the way of doing church since the Protestant Reformation. This, in my mind, is by far the most dramatic new thing God is doing.
—C. PETER WAGNER

SEVEN

The Incredible Shrinking Giant

Now all things are of God, who has reconciled us to Himself through Jesus Christ, and has given us the ministry of reconciliation, that is, that God was in Christ reconciling the world to Himself, not imputing their trespasses against them, and has committed to us the word of reconciliation.
—2 CORINTHIANS 5:18–19

Now to Him who is able to do exceedingly abundantly above all that we ask or think, according to the power that works in us, to Him be glory in the church by Jesus Christ throughout all ages, forever and ever. Amen.
—EPHESIANS 3:20–21

Sir, may I have permission to stop the car?"

As I sat in the back seat of that taxi cab in the Philippines, through the rearview mirror I could see that tears had filled the eyes of the driver. I was attending the Second Lausanne Congress on World Evangelization in Manila. Running a little late for a workshop at a hotel on the other side of the city, I had jumped into the first taxi I could wave down. Realizing that we had about a twenty-minute ride, I took the opportunity to share the gospel with the cab driver.

As I told this man of God's love and Christ's sacrifice for him, I noticed that his eyes had puddled with tears. That's when he asked if he could pull over and talk to me. Turning off the engine, the cab driver turned to face me in the back seat and told me this amazing story.

"In the midst of moral anarchy and spiritual anarchy, how will God's people respond?"

"I don't know if you're going to believe this," he began, "but all night long I've been driving this taxi with a deep, inner ache. This is the last hour of my shift; all last night I drove through the streets of Manila crying out to God. In the last few days there's a phrase that's been haunting me. Maybe I read this phrase, or maybe I heard it on the radio— I don't know. But it keeps going over and over in my mind. Somewhere I heard someone talk about being *born again.*

"All night I've cried, wanting to know what it really means," he continued. "I prayed, 'O God, it would be so wonderful to have a new start in life. I don't know what it means or how it happens. Please put someone in this cab who can tell me how I can be born again!'"

I'm not sure how strategic my presence was at the conference, but I marvel at the Father's tender mercies. I went to the Philippines to "strategize with leading missiologists for world evangelization." God sent me to the Philippines for one seeking cab driver. What a joy it was to see that man pray to receive Christ and to watch him go on his way rejoicing. He experienced the new birth he had desperately sought!

It was so humbling to watch our sovereign God at work, engineering my schedule to intersect with one seeking heart. When I jumped into the first available cab, I wasn't one cab too soon or one too late. This precious experience underscored for me that God is terribly serious about getting the gospel to desperate people. If the church in America is to once again impact culture, we must get in step with the Spirit and get serious about reaching people for Jesus Christ.

George Barna and Mark Hatch pointedly observe, "The Christian church is potentially one of the most powerful agents of influence in our society, but recent decades have seen the impact of the church wane to almost nothing. In fact, the biggest wild card in estimating the future of our country is the church. In the midst of moral anarchy and spiritual anarchy, how will God's people respond?" [1]

That is the big question, isn't it?

THE UNCOMFORTABLE JUNIOR PARTNER

A pretty hot pastor stormed up to me after I had preached in a missions conference. He got close to my face and blurted, "I take strong exception to your statement that the American church is now the junior partner in world missions!" I understood his angst, yet I couldn't help but laugh on the inside. It's just tough on us as Americans to be the junior *anything.*

But that doesn't change the facts.

The facts are that since 1994 more missionaries have been deployed from non-Western nations than Western nations. American Christians now comprise only a small percentage of the global body of Christ. Since 1980 church growth in America has been stagnant while church growth and church planting have burgeoned south of the equator in the same time frame. Although there is strong involvement by American churches in short-term (typically one- or two-week) missions trips, the number of career missionaries from America is in rapid decline. We continue to be a key player in missions because of our economic strength and because we still produce more Christian literature and other Christian media than any other nation. But with the explosive growth of the Internet and the fact that Chinese may soon be the dominant language on the web, our status in these areas is also diminishing.

We cannot be fully effective in evangelism *here* without a commitment to what God is doing globally.

Now, let's balance this out. Although there are great apostolic leaders emerging in developing nations, few of them possess a truly global vision. Their vision, though impressive, usually is only national or at best continental. There are some notable exceptions like David Yonggi Cho who see beyond the evangelization of their own nation to embrace the entire world. But we have not yet seen an African counterpart to Bill Bright, an Asian equivalent to Loren Cunningham or a South American parallel to Pat Robertson. In other words, the United States is still producing the most visionary missions entrepreneurs.

But I believe this is about to change. And if what I've just written provokes a Latin American, African or Asian reader to new missions heights . . . *amen!*

Whether we perceive it or not—whether we *receive* it or not—Western-dominated missions is forever a thing of the past. In this new twenty-first-century context, will the church in America be able to assume a servant role and serve the indigenous leaders and churches God has raised up in many nations? Will we rejoice in indigenous expressions of Christian faith? Will we be able to turn the tide here in the United States, much less continue to be a force in the earth? Andrew Walls reminds us, "The third Christian millennium dawns with the center of gravity of Christianity moving strongly southward toward Africa, Latin America and parts of

Asia. We may expect to see new expressions of Christianity characteristic of these areas as well as a long process of Christian interaction with the ancient cultures of Africa and Asia, parallel to that which earlier centuries saw with those of Greece and Rome and tribal Europe."[2]

Some actually pose this question to me aloud. Many others, I know, are thinking it—"David, we're not even evangelizing our own country. Even in the midst of reports of revival, statistically we're still losing ground. *How can we possibly talk about evangelizing the world?*"

It's a good question—with a good answer. Jesus Himself gives the answer in one of the Great Commission passages: "But you shall receive power when the Holy Spirit has come upon you; and you shall be witnesses to Me in Jerusalem, and in all Judea and Samaria, and to the end of the earth" (Acts 1:8). These are concurrent assignments—one does not exclude the other. In fact, we cannot be fully effective in evangelism *here* without a commitment to what God is doing globally. At the same time, we cannot broad-jump to an unreached people group and carry no concern for our neighbors' salvation. We are to proclaim Christ where we live, beyond our own city, and because we are covenant people, we're also assigned to bless all the families of the earth by bringing the seed of Abraham to them.[3]

It is interesting to note what Jesus did *not* say in the Acts 1:8 commission. He did not say, "Be My witness in the natural traffic patterns of your life." He didn't say, "Reach out to your neighbors, your business associates and your friends." No, He said, "Be My witness in *Jerusalem*—to your entire city!" Then He stretched the disciples' vision even broader, commanding them to reach the ends of the earth. It's as if the Lord were saying, "The very *smallest* terms in which I want you to think is taking whole cities." Jerusalem, at the time of Christ, had a population of approximately four hundred thousand people. I believe a missiological case can be made for strategizing in increments of no less than four hundred thousand people to impact with the gospel. William Carey, the father of the modern missionary movement, caught this extravagant evangelistic spirit, when he challenged the church to "attempt *great* things for God and expect *great* things from God."

It's interesting too that Judea and Samaria are not so much geographic areas as they are descriptions of areas where specific peoples lived. Judea was the area inhabited almost exclusively by Jews, Samaria was inhabited almost exclusively by Samaritans. Again, the Lord is showing us His passionate desire to be known, loved and worshiped by every tribe and people.

The possible merits of protectionism juxtaposed against globalization may be argued in politics, but a protectionist mentality in the church is always suicidal. There are no merits to "spiritual protectionism"; it is always lethal. The most patriotic thing I can do for America is love the world. And the healthiest thing I can do for the American church is to point us beyond ourselves.

One of the best exercises American church leaders could undergo would be to spend a day in prayer, fasting and meditation on the phrase *and not for us only.* If I were president of a Bible college or seminary, I would make it the school motto. The gospel is not for us only. The benefits the gospel brings are not for us only. Jesus is not for us only! "He Himself is the propitiation for our sins, *and not for ours only* but also for the whole world" (1 John 2:2, emphasis added). As Chuck Swindoll said, "Jesus left us a Great Commission, not a limited contract with America."[4]

THE RE-EVANGELIZATION OF AMERICA

Having established our privilege/responsibility to all peoples worldwide, let's look at the very serious challenge of the re-evangelization of America. According to the U.S. Center for World Mission, there are 645 million evangelicals in the world. That's about 11 percent of the world's population.

Clearly, we need a new church—and I *don't* mean new buildings.

Evangelical Christianity is growing worldwide 3.5 times faster than the population, making it the world's fastest-growing religion, but these impressive global statistics do not tell the story of the church in the United States. In the United States the church growth rate (2.2 million annually) has been slightly below the population growth rate (2.6 million). [5]

With every passing day, the United States becomes less homogenous and more compartmentalized, making evangelism more difficult. Our diversity now makes it possible for some children born in America today to live their entire life without a gospel witness.

Yet, thank God, that prospect is still unlikely. Christ-honoring churches continue to dot the landscape of America. And in the midst of some embarrassing para-Bible babble, you can still hear a clear presentation of the gospel through radio and television. Pastor Larry Stockstill differentiates between the *unsaved* and the *unreached*. "People in the United States who are not born again are unsaved," he says, "but they are probably not unreached." They are within earshot of the gospel; the Bible is accessible to them and, to remain unsaved, they must willfully channel surf past gospel programs and drive past evangelical churches. By contrast, people in the 10/40 Window may live their entire lives with no access to the Good News. They are both unsaved and unreached.

We all should be heartened by the new spirit of cooperation

expressed through Mission America.[6] There is a greater level of evangelistic networking among a broader range of Bible-believing Christians than ever in our nation's history. The aggressive proliferation of the *JESUS* video, the participation of thousands in the Lighthouse Prayer Movement and high-profile events among men, women and youth are tremendously encouraging.

Also, there are many churches that are creatively sharing the gospel with postmoderns with wonderful results. Look at the tremendous evangelistic success of Saddleback Community Church, Willow Creek Church and Second Baptist Church of Houston. Hundreds of other churches are experiencing similar strong growth by conversions. In a real sense, they are missionaries to a postmodern generation who have almost as little biblical understanding as an unreached people. Chuck Colson writes, "God calls us to love people enough to go where they are—not only physically but also conceptually. We are to listen to their questions and frame answers they can understand . . . we, as His instruments, are called to love people enough to reach out to them in their own language. This is, of course, what foreign missionaries do; and today, more than ever, we are aliens in our own land, worldview missionaries to our own post-Christian, postmodernist culture."[7]

Also, a quiet revolution has been taking place among Asian Americans. George Barna and Mark Hatch observe that " . . . if there was any degree of spiritual revival during the nineties, it was most likely among Asian-Americans. While 5 percent of Asians were believers in 1991, that figure ballooned to 27 percent in 2000, a 440 percent increase in nine years."[8] (Interestingly, this amazing evangelistic success happened amidst the almost total absence of high-profile Asian-American pastors on radio or television.)

Further, Asian Christians have become a potent missions force to the United States. Acclaimed missiologist Paul Pierson notes, "Mission to the United States today is coming from former 'mission fields' as churches from Asia, Latin America, and, to a lesser extent, Africa, send personnel to minister to immigrants who have come here. The largest group are the Koreans, who have established at least three thousand churches in the United States, and in some cases are beginning to reach out to non-Koreans. The effectiveness of their work is seen in the fact that while 25 percent of the population in Korea is Christian, it is estimated that between 65 percent and 75 percent of Koreans in the United States are Christians."[9]

All of this points to the strong possibility that this could be a very fruitful decade for evangelism in the United States. Again, Barna and Hatch urge us to action:

If ever there was a time for consistent outreach, this is the time. There is a greater level of interest in spiritual matters and in discovering meaning and purpose in life than has been seen at any time in the past fifty years. A large number of people are open to being spiritually mentored by a mature peer. A large majority of born-again Christians believe that they have a responsibility to share their faith in Christ with people they know who are not believers.[10]

Yet in this hopeful climate, the American church is still broadsided by materialism, spending four times as much on buildings and maintenance than on evangelism and follow-up.[11] Clearly, we need a new church—and I *don't* mean new buildings.

NEW DAY—NEW WINESKINS

When the Spirit moves with tornadic strength, there is usually debris to clean up. Old structures are often torn into pieces, and new containers must be made to receive the new move of

God. Jesus taught that new wine requires new wineskins (Matt. 9:17). It is an opportune time for new church structures. Church researchers agree that sociologically in the United States, "it is no longer fashionable for churches to be liturgical,

The fivefold ministry exists to release the church!

traditional, liberal or denominational." [12] Personally, I do not believe God has given up on the historic denominations. Nor should we. Still, as Leonard Sweet has whimsically written, "Denominations could start offering people frequent-flier points to come to church, and they still wouldn't come." [13]

America's "new look" churches need a new brand of leaders at the helm. Fortunately for the American church, there are many strong visionaries serving as pastors. Scripture is clear that "where there is no vision, the people are unrestrained" (Prov. 29:18, NAS). Pastoral leaders with godly vision see God's hand in history and help move the future toward the unrivaled rule of Jesus Christ. Godly vision is not fragile aspirations; it is rock-solid hope anchored in God and His promises. Godly leaders see farther and more clearly than others, and they are compelled to convey what they see to those who follow.

In his landmark book, *The New Apostolic Churches,* Peter Wagner lists nine changes in this new church structure from traditional Christianity. But the most far-reaching of these changes has to do with who actually holds the reins of power in churches. "In my judgment, views of leadership and leadership authority constitute the most radical of the nine changes from traditional Christianity," Dr. Wagner writes. "Here is the main difference: *The amount of spiritual authority delegated by the Holy Spirit to individuals* . . . We are seeing a transition from bureaucratic authority to personal authority, from legal structure to relational structure, from control to coordination and from rational leadership to charismatic leadership." [14]

The Incredible Shrinking Giant

I agree completely. The new generation of charismatic leadership is no longer intimidated by charges of autocracy. This new authority paradigm streamlines the process and allows *rhema* directives given by the Holy Spirit to leaders to quickly become reality. Usually, there are no committees or "feasibility studies" to slow the process. At the same time, there is enormous potential for abuse. This only augments the need for mature leaders who walk humbly before the Lord and before people.

Do we dare hope for church leadership in America that can be prosperous and not flaunt it? By their actions, some leaders infer that the church exists to release the fivefold ministry. This is the exact opposite of what Scripture teaches! The five-fold ministry exists to release the church![15] There is much talk today about apostolic leaders, but what God is really after is an apostolic church. Notice how Paul wove the two together in Romans 1:5–6. In verse 5 he says that he had received from Christ "grace and apostleship to bring about the obedience of faith among all the peoples, for His name's sake" (NAS).[16] Then in the very next verse he says that the entire church has an apostolic function among the nations: "among whom you also are the called of Christ Jesus" (v. 6, NAS).

Only an apostolic church–sent with the gospel–can rescue America from its moral and theological free fall. Because the church has too often failed to be apostolic and prophetic, and because we have too often trivialized Scripture, millions of Americans now seek their advice from late-night TV psychics and other religious quacks. What is the remedy? The Bible is clear:

And when they say to you, "Seek those who are mediums and wizards, who whisper and mutter," should not a people seek their God? Should they seek the dead on behalf of the living? To the law and to the testimony! If they

do not speak according to this word, it is
because there is no light in them.
—Isaiah 8:19–20

There it is—"To the law and to the testimony!" In other
words, *let's get back to the Bible!*

And if Americans remain unrepentant of their occult-
laced paganism, are we bold enough to, like Paul, shake the
dust off our feet and go to the far more responsive nations?
Paul warned of those who were "always learning and never
able to come to the knowledge of the truth" (2 Tim. 3:7).
Some churches are drowning in seminars that produce little
if any life change.

We seldom think of Anglican scholars as prophets, but
Roland Allen was a forward-thinking missions strategist who
was decades ahead of his time. His prophetic words are even
more pungent today than when he wrote them some forty
years ago: "Can there be true teaching which does not
involve the refusal to go on teaching? The teaching of the
Gospel is not a mere intellectual instruction: it is a moral
process, and involves a moral response. If then we go on
teaching where that moral response is refused, we cease to
preach the Gospel; we make the teaching a mere education
of the intellect . . . It is a question which needs serious con-
sideration whether we ought to plant ourselves in a town or
village and continue for years teaching people who deliberately refuse to give us a moral hearing."[17] Perhaps it is time
for thousands of American pastors to stop coddling the carnal and reenlist for ministry as missionaries!

While others may be hesitant regarding evangelism, new
apostolic churches orbit around outreach. "New apostolic
churches focus on outreach," Wagner observes. "Their four
central tasks include 1) church expansion, 2) planting new
churches, 3) mercy ministries and 4) cross-cultural missions."[18] Many of these churches are cell-based churches. We

should not miss the obvious: Currently nineteen out of twenty of the world's largest churches utilize small groups for primarily evangelistic purposes.[19] Clearly the Holy Spirit is showing us an evangelistic method that is right for our times and is effective in many cultures.

For several decades, Elmer Towns has been one of the leading voices on church growth. He has observed how churches grow, particularly in the United States, from the days of aggressive Sunday schools and teams of buses. What does this veteran church-growth analyst see for the new apostolic churches? Dr. Towns writes, "The glue that binds these new [churches and networks] together is the Great Commission, winning people to Christ, worshiping God, small-group Bible studies, energetic worship, gifted leadership and strong personal relationships. These new alliances are held together by the glue of biblical methods, not their particular doctrinal statements nor their traditions."[20]

Hal Sacks, Jim Burkett and others have forged city-wide pastoral relationship networks based not on denominational or even doctrinal affinity, but on a shared hunger for revival and city transformation. Peter Wagner observes, "It is these new extra-denominational alignments in the city where the focus of friendship, commitment, loyalty and mutual accountability are the highest for some pastors."[21] The church's "look" is being overhauled. Why? Because God is about to put His church on display.

CHURCH ON DISPLAY

When God wants to intimidate evil principalities and powers, how does He do it? In a word, He puts His church on display. "To the intent that now the manifold wisdom of God might be made known by the church to the principalities and powers in the heavenly places" (Eph. 3:10).

The word translated *manifold* is the Greek word *polupoikilos*, which literally means "multi-colored or variegated."[22] I am personally convinced that this is a reference to the multi-ethnic composition of the church. If this is so, the implications are breathtaking. Here is a hint as to why God is so adamant that Christ be known and worshiped by every tribe and nation. Literally, when God wants to shut the mouths and halt the taunts of demon spirits, He does so by rubbing in their face the fact that He will receive glory from *all* peoples. His every-people church is the display of His variegated, multi-colored wisdom. This all-peoples, "great-completion" church on display is so dazzling it silences even the fiercest principalities and powers in total defeat!

This is why reconciliation is at the very heart of the missions mandate, and why God has gone to extraordinary lengths in the last several years to bellow this message to His church. We are to be reconciled across denominational, racial, gender and national barriers, demonstrating the true spiritual unity Jesus so passionately prayed for in John 17.

It was a turning point in our hopes for fulfilling the Great Commission when Dr. Avery Willis, representing the International Mission Board of the Southern Baptist Convention, humbled himself in behalf of his denomination before the four thousand delegates to the Global Consultation on World Evangelization in Seoul, Korea. I sat in that crowd of world mission leaders and heard Dr. Willis apologize on behalf of Southern Baptists for sometimes being exclusionists and failing to partner with others. Dr. Willis told the delegates, "We have opened the store."

Dr. Willis' generous act is indicative of a new spirit that is alive and well within the missions community. As a new spirit of partnership emerges among agencies, denominations and mission-hearted Christians around the world, we should be filled with gratitude. God is bringing together all those who carry the missions addiction so that we can produce a global gospel epidemic! Indeed, our only hope of seeing the Great

Commission fulfilled in our lifetime is for all world Christians to link arms to reap the harvest.

God is bringing together all those who carry the missions addiction so that we can produce a global gospel epidemic!

Many trace the beginnings of the Christian ecumenical movement to the Edinburgh Missionary Conference of 1910. That was the first truly interdenominational conference for world evangelization. Sadly, the ecumenical movement progressively lost its missions moorings. But now, a century later, a new ecumenicity is being birthed, not by a compromise of convictions but by a fresh breath of the Spirit among world Christians. We share a common passion for the glory of God and the honor of His Son among all peoples.

Rather than dichotomizing what God has joined together, we embrace a holistic gospel that keeps evangelism paramount while realizing that the effects of the gospel will inevitably lift any culture or nation. In the words of the *Millennial Manifesto,* drafted by the AD 2000 and Beyond Movement, "We reject any dichotomy between church growth and church health, evangelism and social responsibility. While social concern and compassionate service are essential parts of our mission, the primary goal is to make disciples of Jesus Christ, disciples who enter the Kingdom of God through faith and live as His followers now and forever."[23]

Having been reconciled—first to God by faith in His Son, then to one another as brothers and sisters in Christ—we are then called to be ministers of reconciliation. (See 2 Corinthians 5:17–21.) And one of the first fields of conflict is to stand forcibly against any overt or covert racism. As God has grown the church to be a truly global community, all vestiges of racism must now cease.

Jesus attacked the ethnic pride and provincialism of His own disciples by compelling them to travel with Him through Samaria and to interact with the Samaritans. This is an ancient equivalent of asking modern Israelis to walk unarmed through the West Bank and eat, converse with and stay in the homes of Palestinians. It just wasn't done.

Jesus' ministry to the Samaritan woman at the well shows how He lovingly reached across ethnic and gender barriers to meet the needs of this victimized woman. Later, in ministering to the Samaritan villagers, Jesus showed tremendous compassion and quickly accepted the Samaritans' invitation to stay in their village for a few days (much to the chagrin of the disciples!).

Why did Jesus put a full-court press on His disciples to interact with the hated Samaritans? He was kicking the provincialism out of His disciples, assaulting their ethnocentric arrogance and forcing them to live, think and minister in a bigger world. And Jesus continues to do the same with His followers today. He assails our prejudices and kicks the provincialism out of us! If you are going to be Jesus' disciple, you must follow where He leads. And where He is leading is into uncomfortable territory, compelling us to interact with those we may not even naturally like and with whom we share no common heritage. And as we are forced to actually talk to these people, we stop seeing them as "the enemy" and start seeing them as fellow humans who are just as desperate for His touch as we are.

Think of the "crash course" God gave Philip. Little did this deacon in the Jerusalem church realize that he was just weeks away from being launched by God and epochal events to become the church's first cross-cultural evangelist. So how did God prepare this kosher Christian for such an honored assignment? He let him wipe up the slobber from the tables after he had served meals to Greek widows! What's a nice Jewish boy doing with a job like that? God was forcing Philip to deal with the race issue and the gender issue. In essence He was saying to Philip, "Before I give you the incredible honor of showing My Son's power to another culture, I'm going to rid you of any incipient racism or gender bias." And He will do the same with us.

On the beach of Ouidah, Benin, near the mouth of the infamous Gate of No Return where hundreds of Africans were forcibly shipped to the New World as slaves, intercessors from Africa, the Caribbean and the United States renounced the curses of the past and intentionally sought to undo in the Spirit one of history's most horrible crimes against humanity. Something broke loose in the heavenlies that day in December 1999, and a four-hundred-year-old wound began to heal.[24]

Jesus prophesied that one of the telltale signs of His return would be an escalation in ethnic-based hostilities (Matt. 24:7). That's exactly what is tearing our world apart today. Look at the Balkans, Burundi, the Middle East or the inner cities of the United States. The church must rise to the challenge and exhibit the opposite spirit, one of reconciliation. By this the Father is glorified and Jesus is verified. "That they all may be one . . . that the world may believe that You sent Me" (John 17:21).

One way to be a peacemaker is to unilaterally issue forgiveness and to assume responsibility for the sins of our ethnicity, just as Daniel did. Although he was not personally guilty of these particular sins, they were so intertwined with his nation that he felt personal responsibility, and a personal need to repent in the nation's behalf. (See Daniel 9:4–19.) For some, the whole issue of identificational repentance is controversial. However, I believe we should intentionally seek opportunities to humble ourselves before the Lord, the offended and the watching world. John Dawson writes, "Such deep repentance, I'm convinced, not only demonstrates

God's healing love but also robs Satan of ancient strongholds and triggers the harvest. As the Church of Jesus Christ, our goal, of course, has always been to see people reconciled to God through the gospel. The main hindrance to this end, however, has been us."[25]

It's God's hour to display His reconciled and reconciling church. The nations will be magnetically drawn to this glorious church. "Surely you shall call a nation you do not know, and nations who do not know you shall run to you, because of the LORD your God, and the Holy One of Israel; for He has glorified you" (Isa. 55:5).

MOBILIZED FOR MISSIONS

Now it's time for this reconciled, reconciling church to catch the missions addiction. But how, and where, do you start?

I fully agree with Ed Silvoso's assessment that world missions must be at the core of how we view Scripture and how we view the church. Silvoso writes:

I believe the only way to adequately interpret the Scriptures is through the framework of the Great Commission. Every promise, every command in the Bible will be misunderstood (by much or by little) when we fail to interpret it in the light of the Lord's command to win the world for Him. The Bible was written to demonstrate God's love for the lost and His provision for their salvation. Therefore, I contend, the Word can only be fully understood through a missiological grid. God so loved the world that He sent His Son to save it. In order to understand the Son, the Word Himself, we must view Him through His redemptive mission.[26]

Yet so many issues vie for attention in our churches today.

And pastors are overwhelmed. James Engel and William Dyrness have observed that "most biblically based pastors are aware that God is a missionary God. But they also are tugged and pulled in countless directions by other urgencies,

It's God's hour to display His reconciled and reconciling church.

some of which are compelling. Furthermore, there is a constant struggle even in today's most solidly evangelical churches to overcome the pluralistic heresy that Christianity is just one of many equally valid ways to discover God. What this says is that a restoration of missions vision can be an uphill struggle."[27] They go on to suggest that one of the best ways to intensify and focus pastoral support for missions is through "short-term exposure to missions realities." So that is where we should begin. Here are several suggestions to move your congregation toward becoming a world-class church with a missions addiction:

1. EVERY CHURCH, AND ESPECIALLY EVERY PASTOR, SHOULD ANSWER "THE BIG QUESTION."

The big question in missions for every church is, *What unique role has God called this local church to play in helping to fulfill the Great Commission?* God is refocusing His leaders today away from the temporal to the eternal, and beyond a merely local vision to a global one. Any church that is not seriously involved in helping fulfill the Great Commission has forfeited its biblical right to exist. A local church's vision should be intrinsically tied to the greater vision of God's eternal kingdom and the worldwide worship of His Son. The answer to "the big question" does not come, in my opinion, by consensus. It comes by Holy Spirit revelation to the pastor and apostolic leadership of the church. And flowing from the answer, the church can begin to frame its missions policy and determine the distribution of its resources. No matter its size, every church has a unique role to play in missions.

2. THE FIRST ITEM IN ANY CHURCH'S MISSIONS BUDGET SHOULD BE TO SEND THE SENIOR PASTOR IN GENUINE INTERNATIONAL MINISTRY AT LEAST ONCE EVERY YEAR.

The greatest gift any church can sow to the nations is the ministry of their pastor. I'm not talking about attending a conference at an overseas resort. I'm talking about rolling up your sleeves and really pastoring your missionaries, pouring your heart into national pastors, holding starving babies and letting something of God's heart get put into you. This experience will infuse the pastor's ministry at home with a missions dimension.

I agree with Larry Reesor: " . . . regardless of the church polity or structure, the pastor must lead the charge in every area if the local church is to maximize its efforts to reach the world for Christ."[28] And one of the best ways for pastors to get a heart for the world is to get them out into the world beyond a twenty-five-mile radius of their church.

3. EVERY CHURCH SHOULD BECOME, AS JESUS SAID, "A HOUSE OF PRAYER FOR ALL NATIONS."

I'm appealing to every pastor and church leader who is reading: Please make time in each service to pray corporately for nations and unreached peoples! I'm glad that many church auditoriums are now adorned with national flags. Turn those flags into prayer reminders. Also, why not place in your bulletin the name of the nation that is being highlighted that particular day in *Operation World*? Your congregation can join with thousands of others praying on that Sunday (and in the midweek service) for a specific nation on that day.

4. THE CHURCH SHOULD SEEK TO INVOLVE AS HIGH A PERCENTAGE OF ITS PEOPLE AS POSSIBLE IN TEAM MISSIONS.

Obviously God is up to something exciting in local church team missions. Several churches I'm aware of have a stated goal that every able-bodied teenager and adult go on at least one team missions trip! The greatest results of these trips are usually not what the teams accomplish, but rather in what God accomplishes in the teams. Those who get a taste of missions return to their church family as good leaven, kneeding missions passion into the entire church. Many date their missions addiction from a team missions trip. I recently met a businesswoman in her midtwenties. All she does is for the advance of the gospel and the glory of God. She told me that when she was thirteen years old, she took her first missions trip. On the way home, through her tears, she wrote in her diary, "Missions will be my life." Today, it still is.

5. THE CHURCH SHOULD GIVE AT LEAST 10 PERCENT OF ITS INCOME TO MISSIONS AS A MORAL MINIMUM.

I frankly cannot understand how some pastors can so passionately exhort their members to tithe when the church itself doesn't tithe! For almost any church in affluent America, 10 percent to missions should be a moral minimum. Many churches see a tithe of the general income as a starting point, adding faith promises on top of that.

6. REALIZING THAT THE WORLD HAS COME TO US, THE CHURCH SHOULD FORM OUTREACHES TO ETHNIC GROUPS AND INTERNATIONAL STUDENTS IN THEIR AREA.

In my own city there are large contingents of Hispanics, Koreans, Kurds and Indians to mention just a few. Further, most of the world's future leaders are studying in the United States now. And consider this: Several of those future world leaders are probably in close proximity to your church! Are you doing anything to befriend these students? They can be keys to unlock peoples and nations.

7. THE CHURCH SHOULD HONOR, AFFIRM AND SUPPORT MISSIONARIES AND MISSIONARY CANDIDATES.

The true greatness of any church is not in how many it seats but in how many it sends. Churches should joyfully release missionary candidates in their midst to pursue their high calling. What an honor for the sending church to also be the cheering section, encouraging those who go from their church with the gospel.

Churches and missionary-sending agencies should work cooperatively to ensure the strongest care for missionaries. The local, sending church does not have to surrender its pastoral authority to an agency. Conversely, churches are usually poorly equipped to deal with the "nitty gritty" of missionary needs. Patrick Johnstone urges a "three-fold cord" of partnership between training institutions, churches and agencies, and notes that missions' greatest advances are when these three institutions work together.[29]

Some in the church argue against sending young people on missions trips or encouraging them toward career missions. Even some seasoned missionaries warn against an "amateurization" of missions. My question is: Amateur according to *whom?* No doubt Hudson Taylor, Mary Slessor and Cameron Townsend were considered unreasonable young amateurs by some seasoned veterans when they challenged conventional missions patterns. George Verwer reminds us, "Let us older and supposedly more mature leaders acknowledge that many of the so-called quality people of our generation have been knocked out of the battle or fallen into serious sin. The really big mistakes and sins that cause grief to the body of Christ in ways that are hard to assess are not usually those of some inexperienced young person on a short-term mission trip following a call to mobilize."[30]

8. LET'S GET CREATIVE!

The amazing irony is that, while the American church's

role is shrinking in the overall missions drama, the opportunities in missions for individual American Christians are far greater than ever!

Eric Watt is director of the Network for Strategic Missions in Virginia Beach. He stood outside a hotel in China in September 1999 and placed an overseas call on his cellular phone. The operator provided a clear line to the executive of a major ministry in the United States, and Watt explained to his colleague that Chinese businesses had agreed to produce videos and other materials that will be strategic in training fifty million Chinese to plant churches in their country.

"Within days, a model for missions in the new millennium unfolded before my eyes," Watt said. "A massive harvest, local initiatives and global resources all linked together through friendships." Eric Watt represents a new breed of missions strategist who sees not only the validity but the imperative of a symbiotic relationship between American churches, national churches and mission agencies. In this new paradigm, *God* gets the glory, *His church* is expanded and *His kingdom* is extended. In the process, we experience the deep satisfaction of knowing we were a link in God's unfolding drama to bring global fame to His Son. "'No credit, no glory': That must become our standard operating procedure," Watt believes. "And Matthew 24:14–accomplishing the Great Commission–is the goal."[31]

THE SPIRIT OF ADOPTION

In addition to the eight suggestions given above for mobilizing the church for missions, one of the most important steps any body of believers can take is to *prayerfully take ownership of the evangelization of a people group who are currently without the gospel.*

Chuck Warnock, senior pastor of East Texas Church on the

Rock in Longview, Texas, felt compelled by the Holy Spirit in early 1999 that their church should adopt an unreached people. After prayer, the Spirit led them to a major people group in Asia. Although this group numbered some 1.3 million people, little existing research was available at the time.

Later that year the church launched out in faith, taking its first exploratory team to the area. Their hope was merely to find and perhaps make contact with some from this group. Back home the church family prayed fervently every night

"Man's extremities are God's opportunities."

for success. Not only did the team find this people group, but God also engineered opportunities to visit in their homes, eat with them and even to contact several government officials.

When the team returned, they showed a video documenting what God had done. Today, a training school is now preparing young nationals to evangelize and plant viable churches among this group. The clearly stated goal is that in five years they will plant one hundred churches in the region, and within ten years there will be at least sixty thousand believers! This is an example of God-honoring faith based on careful research.[32]

Sometimes, God moves churches to the yet unreached by other routes. Ask Pastor Ron Johnson of Bethel Temple in Hampton, Virginia. In 1999 a vivid dream regarding an unreached people set him on a quest to find them. Through unfolding circumstances that were nothing short of miraculous, Pastor Johnson and a team from his church found and interacted with the very people he so clearly saw in the dream. Today, they are involved in several mercy ministries to this impoverished people of over one million, and the church of Jesus Christ is being planted among them.[33]

The Incredible Shrinking Giant

The American church may be the shrinking giant in missions, but we can still make a world of difference. Jesus has called us into a world of mounting ethnic-based hostilities, an unabated epidemic of AIDS,[34] the deciphering of the genetic code, rogue nations and terrorist groups with weapons of mass destruction, intruding technology to the point that privacy is now considered an obsolete twentieth-century luxury, curious viruses that are resistant to treatment, the disintegration of families, international drug gangs, high-tech slavery, sexual perversion with no limits and increasing ecological calamities.

These global crises spell both danger and abundant opportunity for discerning Christians. Some call it *crisis*—spiritually alert believers should see past the dangers to mega-opportunities for ministry and miracles. Someone observed long ago, "Man's extremities are God's opportunities." The very world itself is on the edge of disaster. What a prime time for God to show up in power!

Now—the question comes home to us: *So what?* What will we *do* in light of the hour God has placed us in history?

Will we sense a stewardship of these colossal opportunities?

Will we pray, think and strategize globally?

Will we live for eternity, realizing that at the Judgment Seat of Christ we must give an account of our stewardship of these momentous days? Or, when we stand before the Lord, will we try to sputter out a reason for being spiritually comatose—"business as usual," through the most hope-filled season of harvest in two thousand years?

There is one more very significant action the American church can take in Third Millennium missions. We can *search out the "no-name foot soldiers" who are truly advancing the gospel among the nations.* Ninety-nine percent of the time it won't be the familiar names of evangelists who fill stadiums. It will be apostolic leaders we've never heard of and humble pastors in the trenches—heaven's hidden heroes.

United States evangelicals will continue to have a significant presence in the twenty-first century, but it will be quite a different missions century. They will continue to bring a significant portion of the resources and support services personnel, but they will not be able to maintain alone their leadership in decision making, expertise, and field personnel. The church in the non-Western world has come into world missions to stay.
—ALEX AERUGO

This is God's message to you—brother, leader, and pastor. The time to preach the gospel to every creature is here! And you have been entrusted with the task. Let's remain firm and united in Christ so together we can see fully the reality that we have only begun to glimpse: the world for Christ.
—CARLOS ANNACONDIA

Yesterday's harvest fields have become today's great harvest forces.
—THE MILLENNIAL MANIFESTO

EIGHT

Hidden Heroes

I was sought by those who did not ask for Me; I was found by those who did not seek Me. I said, "Here I am, here I am," to a nation that was not called by My name.
—Isaiah 65:1

And the things that you have heard from me among many witnesses, commit these to faithful men who will be able to teach others also.
—2 Timothy 2:2

I took a good look at Pastor Javier's feet.

Along with another Tsetsil Indian pastor, Javier had walked three days through the mountains of Chiapas, Mexico, to attend our Frontline Shepherds Conference. Like most of the Third World pastors Global Advance is privileged to serve, Javier had no formal training for ministry. But having heard that there was ministry training in his area, he thought it was worth a three-day walk.

I watched Javier throughout the conference. Sometimes he would just drink in the teaching with a big smile. At other times, he was feverishly taking notes. Sometimes, he would just silently weep as God's Spirit ministered to him through the training sessions.

I believe the single greatest key to world evangelization lies in the empowering of indigenous leaders.

Now at the end of the conference he came up to me to say thanks. He did not speak English or Spanish, and I didn't speak his Tsetsil dialect. So he thanked me for the training in a more profound way—he just put his head on my chest and cried.

As I embraced this precious brother, I looked down at his feet. They were still swollen from the three-day walk. They were dusty and calloused. Their only protection was a pair of thin moccasins that appeared to be hand-sewn. I looked again and remembered, "How beautiful upon the mountains are the feet of him who brings good news; who proclaims peace, who brings glad tidings of good things, who proclaims salvation" (Isa. 52:7).

I dedicate this chapter to the church's hidden heroes—pastoral leaders like Javier, those I call *frontline shepherds* in developing nations. Against all odds and the very forces of hell they courageously advance the gospel. Their faith mirrors the faith of the early church in the Book of Acts. Like the first Christian believers, their financial resources are often limited at best. Like those early Christians, they honor Christ in the midst of pagan rituals and hostility. Like many believers in the early church, martyrdom is a constant, real possibility. And, as Bruce Wilkinson says, "like those Christians in the Book of Acts–[they] look at who they are and who they'll never be, and what they can do now and what they'll never be able to do . . . and still ask God for the world."[1]

WHY WE EQUIP NATIONAL LEADERS

Amos Phiri had pastored a small congregation of some fifty people in the interior of Zambia when he came to Global Advance's first Frontline Shepherds Conference there in 1993. Like most of the Third World pastors we're privileged to serve, Pastor Phiri had no formal training for ministry. I watched him throughout the conference as he drank in the training on evangelism, church growth and church planting. I knew God was stirring this man's heart.

Two years later, Pastor Phiri returned to our second conference in Zambia. He shared with me that the vision and training he received at our previous conference launched him from pastoring one rural church to being a church planter. In fact, in the ensuing two years, Pastor Phiri had planted fourteen new churches in Zambia, Malawi and Mozambique! He just took the cross-cultural, Bible-based teaching from our conference and ran with it! Pastor Phiri told me, "You may think what you are teaching us is simple, but for us it is life-changing." God reconfirmed to my heart once again how strategic it is to equip hidden heroes like Pastor Phiri if we're going to see closure on world evangelization.

The Great Commission of our Lord is very clear. What has not been so clear is the strategy that should be employed to fulfill this command. Many missions methods have been tried. Most methods have some merit and have been fruitful to some degree, and each method also has its limitations.

Ours is a world of some six billion people with growing global antagonism to sustained foreign missionary presence. It is incumbent upon the church to prayerfully seek the best method that is also a biblical method for obeying Christ's commission in light of the realities of today's world.

There is such a strategy, one that transcends both time and cultures. I believe the single greatest key to world evangelization lies in the empowering of indigenous leaders. As national church leaders receive relevant training, effective tools and the touch of God's Spirit, they are then enabled to reach their nations and nearby unreached peoples, strengthen existing churches and plant new ones. Further, these indigenous pastoral leaders assume a new role of leadership in the body of Christ, and their churches are transformed from a missions field to a missions force.

The apostle Paul employed this method of multiplying effectiveness. As a mentor to Timothy, he counseled him, "And the things you have heard from me among many witnesses, commit these to faithful men who will be able to teach others also" (2 Tim. 2:2). Paul knew that the best way to multiply the church was through entrusting truth to reliable leaders who would, in turn, share these truths with others.

The great new fact of new millennium missions is the internationalization of the church. Now in almost every nation there are capable, indigenous leaders. But so often they are limited—limited in training, limited in exposure to the larger body of Christ and almost always limited by a lack of effective tools to reach their own people with the gospel. Yet these pastoral leaders are the single greatest key to the evangelization of their respective nations. These frontline shepherds are truly the hidden heroes of the Christian mission. These committed servants of Jesus Christ are shepherding God's flock on the very frontlines of the gospel's advance in nation after nation, often amidst persecution and with precious little training or encouragement.

It just makes good sense to invest in equipping these frontline shepherds. They are, of course, the *quickest way* to reach a nation. They are already in the white harvest fields. While more and better training is their greatest need, they don't have to halt their ministries and spend long years in a seminary thousands of miles away from their people and calling. Although this is sometimes productive, taking a native pastor out of his nation for extended periods often works in reverse. Instead of being better equipped to serve his people, he is often perceived as elite and no longer capable of identifying with the struggles of his own people. That is why on-the-job-training is the best option for most indigenous pastors.

Further, frontline shepherds are the most *cost-effective* way to reach a nation. They don't have to live at Western standards of affluence. They don't have to go home for a furlough—they *are* home, ministering to people they know and love.

A man recently wanted to know more about the ministry I serve. "So Global Advance trains national leaders?"

"That's our calling," I responded.

"So you believe in supporting national leaders?"

"No," I responded, "I believe in *equipping* national leaders and truly partnering with them."

I went on to explain that I view equipping national church leaders much the same way that I see my equipping responsibility to my sons. I invested a significant amount of money in their education—their training—for the expressed purpose that they would *not* be dependent on me in the future. To "support" national workers with guaranteed income from us defeats the indigenous principle. In fact, there's a vigorous discussion right now among missiologists on the effects of Western money on Third World churches.[2]

What is healthy is true partnership. We give as we are prompted by the Holy Spirit. But there is no "umbilical cord" of dependency. National church leaders want true indigenous status, and they deserve it. An indigenous church is self-governing, self-supporting, self-propagating and self-missionizing. In other words, the church in non-Western nations must be able to stand on its own feet financially. Otherwise, it will not have the strength to be "self-missionizing"—it will be too weak to be a missionary sending force itself.

Again, this does not mean that we in the West who have

strong financial resources are insensitive to the needs and opportunities true partnership brings. It simply means that we renounce all paternalism, invest in equipping and then continue to give as the Spirit directs.

The acclaimed Assemblies of God missionary Melvin Hodges saw both the problem of paternalism and the potential of affirming partnership half a century ago. He stated flatly, "To proceed on the assumption that the infant church in any land must always be cared for and provided for by the mother mission is an unconscious insult to the people that we endeavor to serve and is evidence of a lack of faith in God and in the power of His Gospel."[3] Hodges first penned those words in 1953. How much more potent is his observation in today's world.

> It's imperative that we act now, that we move strategically and that we minister with strength to empower these deserving hidden heroes.

We need to revisit this wise advice, given by one of the foremost Pentecostal missionaries. Years of experience convinced him that " . . . our problem lies in the *failure to work for an indigenous church*. Unless a church can be taught the necessity of shouldering its own burden and facing its own problems, it cannot be expected to develop even with the aid of periodic revival outpourings." Decades ago Donald McGavran crafted a breakthrough missiology, insisting that church planting and church growth be adapted to culture. And he made this insistence in a time when Western missionaries—and too often Western attitudes—were considered incontrovertible. Whatever we as the Western church do to assist the church in developing nations, it should foster the indigenous principle, not work against it.

Finally, frontline shepherds are the most *culturally sensitive* way to reach a nation. They already know the language; they're part of the culture. They share the hopes and aspirations of the people they serve. That's why Global Advance goes to these deserving leaders with Frontline Shepherds Conferences and Global Advance Institutes, bringing training, resources and encouragement directly to them on the front lines of spiritual combat. We're committed to the goal of equipping one million pastoral leaders, especially in developing nations, and challenging them to plant one million new churches. This is a doable vision in our lifetime!

In the last decade God handed the church one of the greatest miracles in history. Doors swung open to entire nations that had been shut tight to the gospel. But God only knows how long these doors will remain open to Western missions. If the doors to our involvement were to close again, who would remain? The national church and its indigenous leaders.

It's imperative that we act now, that we move strategically and that we minister with strength to empower these deserving hidden heroes. God has brought them to their nations and us to their aid "for such a time as this." Just as Aaron and Hur lifted up Moses' hands and thus secured victory for God's people, we too can "lift up the hands" of the church's hidden heroes by our prayers and our investing in equipping them.

What's preventing an even greater global harvest? In a word, we need more and better servant-leaders in the body of Christ. Berin Gilfillan is right: "The bottleneck in the harvest is leadership, and the bottleneck in leadership is old wineskins."

In his apostolic function, Paul taught an intensive two-year discipleship course for committed students in the school of Tyrannus. The result was that "all who dwelt in

Asia heard the word of the Lord Jesus, both Jews and Greeks" (Acts 19:10). That's the phenomenal impact training can have—if you have the right students and the right curriculum. Commenting on this amazing effect of intensive training for church leaders, Peter Wagner writes:

> Luke seems to suggest a cause-and-effect relationship between [Paul's leadership training] and the fact that "all who dwelt in Asia heard the word of the Lord Jesus" (v. 10) before the end of two years. This means that the chief focus of the curriculum was likely to have been evangelism and church planting.
>
> Paul, then, was training and sending out church planters as rapidly as he could. This is not to be seen as a deviation in Paul's ministry from evangelism to Christian nurture. Paul was not hereby falling into the trap of the "syndrome of church development," which I have mentioned from time to time . . . his priority would likely have been to train the pastoral leaders God had selected and to put special emphasis on church planters.
>
> Modern missionaries should take their direction from Paul's example . . . The great missionary challenge . . . is not so much evangelism as it is leadership selection and training. Many of the new converts will be weak Christians or drawn back into the world without the vigorous multiplication of churches under trained leadership.
>
> By trained leadership, I do not necessarily mean those who have college and seminary degrees. The number of church planters who have such academic credentials is minuscule in

proportion to the number of new churches
being planted each day around the globe. By
"training leadership" I mean doing what Paul
was apparently doing in Ephesus—taking gifted
believers, whoever they might be, with whatever education they might have, providing for
them the conceptual and practical tools they
need, and sending them out to extend the
kingdom of God. It paid off then, and such a
training design will pay off now.[4]

For the last eleven years we've watched it pay off at Global
Advance as we've gone to tens of thousands of the church's
hidden heroes for the expressed purpose of putting a vision
in their hearts and tools in their hands.

HATS OFF TO HIDDEN HEROES

The great new missions' fact of our time is the internationalization of the church and ownership of the Great Commission by the body of Christ worldwide. In the last one
hundred years, according to the newly published second
edition of the *World Christian Encyclopedia*, the racial makeup
of Christian believers has changed dramatically from 81 percent white in 1900 to 55 percent nonwhite in 2000.[5]

The twenty-first-century missionary force from developing
nations is sometimes poor, but almost always spiritually
radical and therefore juxtaposed to the wealthy, conservative
church of the West. The new missions force is much more in
touch with poverty, oppression and the supernatural. This
will inevitably have a profound effect on global Christian
theology and missiology in the decades ahead.

This new look of the twenty-first-century church is only
now beginning to be noticed. Philip Jenkins notes that
" . . . the largest Christian communities on the planet are to
be found in Africa and Latin America, and if we want to

visualize a 'typical Christian,' we should think of a woman living in a village in Congo or a shantytown in Brazil. But this Southern emphasis is nothing compared with what we should see in forty or fifty years, since the regions of most rapid Christian expansion also happen to include the nations with the fastest-growing populations."

Jenkins further assets that the day of North American dominance of Christianity is over: "That era has passed within our lifetimes. And so little did we notice this momentous change that it was not once mentioned in all the media hoopla surrounding the end of the second millennium. The numerical changes are striking enough, but the implications for Christian belief are only beginning to be apparent . . . God is not only burningly alive across the planet, He promises to be ever more obviously and immediately so. Inevitably, too, these new currents will transform Christianity in the advanced countries of the global North, as waves of immigrants import the vibrant Christianity of Africa and Latin America."[6] Indeed this is happening very dramatically right now in London, where the senior pastors of the city's two largest churches are men from Nigeria and Peru.

Ninety-five percent of the two million church leaders in developing nations have not had the opportunity of formal training for ministry in a Bible school or seminary. But they're out there on the front lines of spiritual combat just the same, slugging it out with little training and few resources. Their desperate cry is for encouragement in the battle, relevant on-site training and resources for ministry.

I think, for instance, of the astounding proliferation of evangelical churches throughout Brazil, most of them started and sustained without money from outside. Danny Rollins, Southern Baptist missionary to Brazil, notes, "The Assemblies of God have a church in every neighborhood. As soon as they can, they will get a man out there. He might not have much training, but he will be there trying to start a church."[7]

I've seen this firsthand. Church planting seems to be in the spiritual DNA of the Brazilian church and its leaders. One young pastor I met in central Brazil founded his first church five years ago, both as a local church *and* as a leadership training center for new pastors. Since then, this apostolically gifted pastor has planted an astounding fifty-nine churches!

I want to lock arms with men like that. They are the church's hidden heroes—godly servant-leaders in the trenches of the gospel's advance around the world. They are crafting a new leadership paradigm for the twenty-first-century church. These self-effacing leaders possess anointing without arrogance, boldness without brashness and power without pride.

Lee Grady, editor of *Charisma* magazine, recently contacted several underground churches in China. He returned with this report:

The humility of my new Chinese friends exposed my pride. Their childlike faith revealed how much I trust in technology, education and the idols of Western materialism. Their infectious passion to fulfill the Great Commission forced me to see my self-centeredness.

I've had enough of our abnormal, Americanized brand of Christianity. It is as impotent as it is lethal. After spending time with my brothers and sisters in China, I've realized that some of what I see in the church (and even what is reflected in the pages of this magazine) makes God sick.[8]

Indeed, as we interact with our brothers and sisters from the Third World, we realize that teaching and impartation is very much a two-way street. The cultural gifting of Americans is to impart vision. But how very much we have to learn in the "school of humility" as we sit at the feet of Christians from developing nations. Paul understood that when believers inter-act from different cultures the benefit goes both ways. He told the church in Rome, "I long to see you, that I may impart to you some spiritual gift, so that you may be established." Then immediately he acknowledged that he would receive from them as well: " . . . that I may be encouraged together with you by the mutual faith both of you and me" (Rom. 1:11–12).

"Bring the gospel to us as a seed, not as a potted plant!"

It has been suggested by some that the new role of American Christians in missions is simply to sponsor mission projects overseas and help fund the younger, more vibrant church in developing nations. While I agree that partnership certainly includes a financial element, I believe it mocks true partnership simply to throw money at our brothers and sis-ters in developing nations. Far more important to them than money is our affirmation, our prayers and ongoing relation-ships. They are deeply grateful for training and resources from us, provided that it is given with a servant's heart and that the training is not Westernized but truly cross-cultural.

Let's receive from one another. Partnering together can become our strongest asset for reaping the greatest possible harvest. Grant McClung challenges us:

Let's globalize the doctrinal process and ask Asian-Indian Pentecostals to help us with the New Age Movement (reworked Hinduism, customized for a European and American audience). Let's get Asian, African and Latin American pastors and evangelists on our Bible conference and retreat programs to talk to us about spiritual warfare, signs and wonders, and "power evangelism." Let's continue to encourage faculty exchanges with the "third church" to learn about theology through Third-World eyes. Let's call for the aggressive missionary evangelists from the burgeoning Third-World Pentecostal churches to "come over to Macedonia and help us."[9]

That's why biblical principles are so valuable. Scripture itself is cross-cultural. Let's remember that *we* received the Bible from Middle Eastern Hebrew writers! Yes, every culture must contextualize its message to some degree. But the power is not so much in contextualization, the power is in the gospel itself.

Too often we have taken the precious seed of the gospel, allowed it to bloom in America soil, then we've sprayed it with American-made chemicals and disinfectants that have thwarted its growth. Then, to make things worse, we've taken this Americanized plant, potted it, kept it in our soil and transported it. As one African pastor appealed to his American friends, "Bring the gospel to us as a seed, not as a potted plant!"

THE NEW MISSIONS FORCE

The non-Western church is learning to brush away the Western soil and keep the precious seed. These new churches are now producing vast indigenous missionary movements. In fact, David Bryant states that the non-Western missions movement is growing five times faster than that of the West.[10]

I saw the effect of indigenous missions in a recent trip to Turkey. I met men from Iran, Spain, Guatemala and the United States who are serving as "workers" in Istanbul. The worker from the United States was a Muslim who had immigrated from Turkey to the States as a young man. He eventually came to Christ through the ministry of Second Baptist Church in Houston. Later, he was powerfully impacted in charismatic revival meetings. As a result of this touch of

God's Spirit, he felt called to return to Turkey. Today, he pastors one of the country's largest churches.

I'm writing this chapter from a hotel room in Douala, Cameroon. I'm here to minister at a national missions conference sponsored by Discipling the Nations Ministries, founded by a gifted young apostolic leader, Hal Rahman. Pastor Rahman, who is from Sierra Leone, met his wife, who is Liberian, when they were students in Bible school in Liberia some twenty years ago. They felt called as missionaries to Cameroon. And what an impact this apostolic missionary couple is making in Cameroon and across Francophone Africa. In the last sixteen years they have been instrumental in planting dozens of churches, and they have founded Bible schools that meet in fifteen different locations throughout Cameroon. Their focus is on sending their graduates to do research and church planting among the Muslim peoples of North Africa.

I love the requirements for their students. Along with successful completion of classroom courses, in the first year each student is required to win at least fifteen people to Christ through his or her personal witness. Before graduating in their second year, students are required to begin a cell group with fifteen people. Many who comprise these cell groups are converts from the previous year. At graduation, several students stay with these groups they have begun and grow them into cell-based churches. Others raise up a leader for their cell group and go to an unreached people.

This is consistent with the level of commitment I've seen in many Bible schools on every continent. Over the last several years I've ministered in dozens of schools in response to God's call for me to impart missions passion to the upcoming generation. It's an honor to pass on the missions addiction. I think of the Bible school in Singapore where most of the students anticipate being martyred in China, or the Assemblies of God school in Brazil where the entire student body wants to plant churches among unreached peoples. I remember the night a few years ago when I prayed and laid my hands on hundreds of students at Christ For The Nations in Dallas as they responded to my call to missionary service.

Then there is the Bible school in the Batam province of Indonesia. The dean told me that the requirements for graduation are not academic as much as they are spiritual. In addition to successfully completing the courses of study, each student must sign a pledge that he or she is willing to be persecuted and even die for Christ. Then they must recount their personal call and vision to a specific city or people group. Finally, they must actually go and establish a cell group with a view to multiplying into a church. Only then are they awarded a diploma!

It just makes good sense to partner with apostolic leaders in developing nations and the churches they have established. Who, for instance, is in the best position—culturally and geographically—to reach the nine million Uygurs in China, where there are only fifty known Christians among them? Apostolically gifted leaders and churches in Asia—if not the only hope of reaching them—are certainly the best hope.

Howard Foltz, founder of Advancing International Mission Strategies (AIMS) writes, "The churches in the West will be wise to learn how to partner with churches in developing nations for cooperative ventures to reach 'third-party' groups of unreached peoples. If we do not learn how to do this we will be left behind, because God is dancing on the grave, so to speak, of the colonial approach to missions work. He is going on with partnership strategies and cross-cultural teamwork."[11]

Third World apostolic leaders seem to know instinctively what produces church growth, and they're teaching these principles to their students. What are the factors that are producing such vigorous church growth in developing nations? Why, for instance, are there more people worshiping on any given

Sunday in evangelical churches throughout Latin America than in Roman Catholic churches? Rigoberro Galvez, director of the Neo-Pentecostal Seminary of Guatemala, provides the answer as to why Third World churches, especially Pentecostal and charismatic churches, are thriving: "Pentecostal churches have practical leadership, live in fraternal love, and do not inhibit their emotions . . . They are aggressive in evangelism and practice freedom in worship."[12]

With Peter Wagner and many other missions observers, I believe that no missiological principle is more important than church planting.[13] And today's apostolic leaders in developing nations aren't just planting new churches; they're spawning entire church planting movements. In his excellent book, *Apostolic Strategies Affecting Nations,* Jonathan David writes, "Antioch became an apostolic center that provided many apostolic initiatives across the various regions. From Antioch to Rome the apostolic work spread through the tireless efforts of Paul and his companions. When a whole church takes upon itself an apostolic burden to reach their regions and beyond, a new breakthrough of apostolic endeavor is on the horizon. The church at Antioch gladly gave up two of its best men for apostolic work."[14]

And the church throughout the Third World is gladly doing the same. Just one hundred ten years ago there were no known Christians in Korea. But today the city of Seoul, Korea, is home to seven of the world's ten largest churches! Further, South Korea has sent seven thousand missionaries to one hundred forty-five nations. "We pray that we will be the last marathon runners of the gospel for the last tribes," says John Ko, general secretary of the Korean Mission Council.[15]

The church, especially in developing nations, is rising to the occasion to reap history's greatest harvest. John Eckhardt issues this call to the church in every nation: "God is calling His Church to step out of mediocrity and into the fullness of its calling and heritage, that the Great Commission might finally be fulfilled and the glorious return of Christ realized. But that will only happen through the restoration of the apostolic ministry and an aggressive appropriation of all that means to the End-Time Church."[16]

> **"When a whole church takes upon itself an apostolic burden to reach their regions and beyond, a new break-through of apostolic endeavor is on the horizon."**

In recent years, not only has God been restoring an apostolic *company*, He's been restoring an apostolic *church*. Let's remember that the restoration of the fivefold ministry is not the point. That is the means to an end. The end result God is after is a full-grown church that is ministering in apostolic authority—believers ("saints," as Paul calls them) who are equipped for ministry (Eph. 4:11–12).

Paul said he personally had "received grace and apostleship" for the expressed purpose of bringing the nations to faith in Christ for the glory of His name. Then he extends that apostolic, missionary authority in the next verse to the entire church: "Among whom [i.e., among the nations] you also are the called of Jesus Christ" (Rom. 1:5–6). Not only was Paul called by Christ with an apostolic anointing for the nations, but also the entire church was to go in apostolic authority!

10/40, 40/70 AND GOD'S SURPRISES

So I'll be blunt. Nairobi doesn't need any more Western missionaries—not unless they are based there for the expressed purpose of getting to unreached peoples and areas. We should leave the maturing of the indigenous church up to the indigenous churches.

God has young people hidden in His quiver who will emerge in the twenty-first century as great international leaders of the body of Christ. One of them may be reading this book right now.

It's time to let the younger churches do their job of discipling their nations. And then it's time to link arms with them as the global missions force for this new century. As veteran missionary to the Amazon region, Steve Saint, observed, "Hidden peoples from 'Jerusalem to Irian Jaya' are waiting to fulfill their role in God's Great Commission. If we could grasp the vision of what the Holy Spirit wants to do through them, we western missionaries could move on to the hundreds of places where there are no indigenous believers and missionaries are truly needed."[17]

Rumblings of the Spirit are being felt across the newly defined "40/70 Window." The Balkans, Turkey, northern China and the area formerly known as the Soviet Union are ripe for spiritual harvest. Further, there are still multiplied millions representing peoples in the 10/40 Window who will live and die without the gospel unless we dispatch more missionaries. All of this points to the need for a vastly enlarged missions force in this decade, comprised of an apostolic company from both Western nations and developing nations.

Luis Bush reminds us, "The 10/40 Window continues to

represent the primary geographic challenge entering the twenty-first century. By 2025 there will be over 8.3 billion people in our world. Over a billion will need cross-cultural witness to understand the gospel, most of whom will live in the 10/40 Window. It is the geographical location in which the concentration of the main spiritual, ideological, social, urban, people group challenges are most prominent. There are an estimated 1.2 to 1.4 billion people who have never had the chance to hear the gospel, and over 95 percent of these individuals reside in the Window area. It is where 85 percent of the world's poorest and most deprived live. It is the residence of over 95 percent of the Muslims, Hindus and Buddhists in the world. Many of the world's least-reached peoples live in this area. From the Joshua Project 2000's List of Unreached Peoples there are still 249 large groups that remain unclaimed, with no agencies reportedly planning to send workers to them; 542 of them currently have no church planting team on-site; and 1,107 are without a congregation of at least 100 believers."[18]

So, is the day of mass evangelism over? Hardly! Just ask Reinhard Bonnke, Benny Hinn or scores of evangelists in developing nations whose names you haven't heard. They are seeing open-air crowds that are larger than any of the historic crusades of earlier decades. Nevertheless, large-scale evangelistic meetings are already being eclipsed by apostolic church planting as the Holy Spirit's "preferred method" of evangelization for the years ahead.

Still, there will need to be a "Billy Graham" for this new century, not so much in the role of an evangelist as in the role of one who models all that is best and most Christ-honoring in evangelicalism. Further we will need someone with sufficient catalytic strength to convene us for major world evangelization events in the future, as Mr. Graham and his organization have done in the past. Mr. Graham has served as a standard bearer and model for evangelicals the world over. Although his ministry will not be duplicated,

God will unveil a new expression of men and women to once again raise the bar and set the standard for the twenty-first century. I believe there may be literally dozens of high-impact international ministries on the order of Billy Graham in the days ahead. I doubt that many of them will be from the Western church. Right now, God has young people hidden in His quiver who will emerge in the twenty-first century as great international leaders of the body of Christ. One of them may be reading this book right now.

In this respect, David Yonggi Cho has been something of a John the Baptist. More and more in the days ahead, Western church leaders will sit at the feet of apostolically gifted men and women from developing nations to be instructed by them in the dynamics of sacrifice, evangelism, worship, spiritual warfare and birthing church planting movements.

A true "fivefold ministry" is developing throughout the churches of the Third World, and this is vastly accelerating the gospel's advance. In recent years, Peter Wagner has been a strong advocate for a restoration of all the ministry gifts to the church for the specific purpose of closure on the Great Commission. Dr. Wagner notes, "The amazing thing is that even though for centuries we had the order of the church backwards, God has done wonderful things through the church, including the spreading of the gospel of Christ to virtually every major people group on the face of the earth. Just imagine what we can look forward to now that things are beginning to come back together in proper biblical order."[19]

When thousands of church leaders gathered for Amsterdam 2000, the overwhelming majority represented developing nations. Leaders from the younger churches of the southern hemisphere and Asia were primarily responsible for drafting the statement that would echo the commitment of the delegates. Their statement, The Amsterdam Declaration, reiterates a resolve for both the fulfilling the Great Commission and the global worship of Christ in the context of indigenous churches. The delegates who signed this Declaration made this commitment:

We pledge ourselves to work so that all persons on earth may have the opportunity to hear the gospel in the language they understand, near where they live. We further pledge to establish healthy, reproducing, indigenous churches among every people, in every place, that will seek to bring to spiritual maturity those who respond to the gospel message.

This commitment will be carried out in a climate that is unfavorable to its success. With rare exceptions, gone are the days when the tribal chief warmly welcomed the incoming missionary. If we merely wish to "hold our own," there will not be much opposition. But if we would advance, we will draw enemy fire.

The records of evangelism from the apostolic age, the state of the world around us today, and the knowledge of Satan's opposition at all times to the spread of the gospel, combine to assure us that evangelistic outreach in the twenty-first century will be an advance in the midst of opposition.
—THE AMSTERDAM DECLARATION

We abandon ourselves unreservedly to Him and to His cause. In doing so, we know we will risk incurring the wrath of a world that rejects us even as it rejected and crucified Him. Yet His Great Commission is not merely an option to be considered but a mandate to be obeyed. Therefore, in light of His Second Coming, we covenant together, by God's enabling grace, to strive toward the goal of the whole church taking the whole Gospel to the whole world.
—THE MILLENNIAL MANIFESTO

Your core values are a reflection of what you will suffer for.
—FLOYD MCCLUNG

NINE

Siege on
the Saints

*Who shall separate us from the love of Christ? Shall tribulation, or
distress, or persecution, or famine, or nakedness, or peril, or sword?
As it is written: "For Your sake we are killed all day long; we are
accounted as sheep for the slaughter." Yet in all these things we are
more than conquerors through Him who loved us. For I am
persuaded that neither death nor life, nor angels nor principalities
nor powers, nor things present nor things to come, nor height nor
depth, nor any other created thing, shall be able to separate us from
the love of God which is in Christ Jesus our Lord.*
—ROMANS 8:35–39

*Remember that Jesus Christ, of the seed of David, was raised from
the dead according to my gospel, for which I suffer trouble as an evil-
doer, even to the point of chains; but the word of God is not chained.*
—2 TIMOTHY 2:8–9

The church is under fire because the church is advancing. In the wake of the church's advance, ancient
strongholds are being uprooted and long-held ideolo-
gies are toppling. Effective evangelism invariably draws fire.

Very often the ministry of Jesus leads to arenas of pain and
violence because He has always given priority to the weak
and wounded. At the 1996 Urbana Mission Conference,
missionary to Afghanistan Libby Little shared the following
testimony:

**In Acts 8:26 we read, "The Spirit directed
Philip to go to a place and stay near"** . . .

181

Our family was called to Afghanistan, and we were called to stay near. That was twenty years ago, and we're still there . . . I am trembling as I recall the times that God called us to stay and not leave the place of suffering . . .

It did not take long for the glamour of missions to wear off. The memory of the applause of friends back home was soon drowned out by the thunder of MiGs bombing the city where we lived, the terrified screams of children on the street and the last whimpering cries of the slaughtered just houses away. During the first lull in the fighting, an evacuation convoy was arranged for all foreigners. We struggled, my husband and I, to hear if God might be calling us to a safer place. No, the call to stay remained the same. The evacuation convoy came and left without us. Our neighbors were puzzled. Later we heard them call us no longer "the foreigners," but "the people who stayed."

During our first Christmas there we learned the full impact staying had on the community. Over fifty women and their children all squeezed into our home, a little living room, to hear the advent story. Some wept. Some of them wept hearing it the first time. Others ran to their husbands and told them to go to the house of "the people who stayed" and hear the Good News.

During the next fifteen years of civil war, two of our team members were murdered. Colleagues were tortured. Our homes were hit with rockets. The hospital where my husband worked was completely destroyed. The front line of battle moved to our neighborhood streets...There were robberies, attempted rapes, beatings and threats to our fellow team members.

Perhaps for me as a mother of three daughters, the hardest part of staying was always to trust God daily for the safety of our children . . . I confess I often wanted to escape the seriousness and sadness of war. Just last Christmas I frittered away a whole day putting up decorations, trying to ignore all the sounds outside our door. But that evening, however, someone came to our gate. Before I even saw who was there I felt Jesus say, "Put all of that away and make room for Me." There at our door was a family of nine. They were covered with splinters of glass, shrapnel bits and soot. The blood on their faces told of their narrow brush with death when a rocket had hit their home. They had come to stay with us. I tell you, that night when Jesus touched their pain and their suffering with His mercy, the Holy Spirit filled us with joy . . .

We will return to Afghanistan in a few weeks to join a team of international Christians called to do medical development and relief work to the glory of God. Each of us knows that obedience to God does not mean immunity from suffering. "Staying near" may involve injury, even loss of life. We believe that Jesus would say in His kingdom there are things worth dying for.[1]

HIGH-RISK CHRISTIANITY

Christians around the world are no strangers to harassment,

persecution and even martyrdom. Some time ago, in a hotel in Africa, I met with a leader of the network of underground churches in a very repressive nation. He shared with me remarkable stories of how the gospel is advancing in the most adverse circumstances. Finally I asked him, "What is your number-one prayer request?"

He didn't ask for money. He certainly didn't want notoriety; that would put him and many others at even higher risk. His number-one prayer request: "Pray that all the brothers and sisters will be strong and that no one will defect from the faith."

"We believe that Jesus would say in His kingdom there are things worth dying for."

This church leader went on to tell me of the tremendous pressure put on Christians in that nation if they are caught. Often the authorities will present the captured Christian with an option like this: "Just tell us the names and addresses of those in your cell group, and we'll give you $5,000 in cash [a larger sum of money than most believers in that nation have ever seen]. Keep silent, and we'll send you to prison for five years." God's Word tells us, "Remember the prisoners as if chained with them—those who are mistreated—since you yourselves are in the body also" (Heb. 13:3). There are thousands in prison today for the sole "crime" of their witness for Christ.

But persecution often backfires. Take the case of Ado Umar, a former radical Muslim in Nigeria. Several years ago he went to an evangelistic crusade armed with petrol, kerosene and swords to disrupt the meeting. The Muslim imam had encouraged him toward violence. After all, Ado was one of the top recruits of this particular Islamic sect. "This is your chance to show this community that the money we have invested in you is not in vain," the Muslim clergyman told him. "We have learned that a Christian group is coming to this village to preach. Your task is to ensure that this doesn't happen." Instead, arrested by the preacher's message, later that night Ado gave his life to Christ. Today, amidst angry threats from Muslims and former friends, he pastors a church in northern Nigeria with the Evangelical Church of West Africa.[2]

Of course, there are the multiple stories coming out of China telling of a strong, young church that is thriving in the face of intense opposition. Chinese church leader Jonathan Chao estimates that there are between 63 million and 83 million Christians in China. This makes China the nation with the most Christians. The unregistered house churches in China that refuse to come under the authority and restrictions of the government are seeing an estimated 8 million people turn to Christ every year.[3] They are a major part of the phenomenal evangelistic success that is seeing some 28,000 people receive Christ in China every day!

While Christians in general are often harassed in China, the full wrath of the communists is reserved especially for young Christians and church-planting pastors. Heavy fines, imprisonment and torture are often the consequences for advancing the gospel.[4] On September 4, 2000, Liu Hautao, a nineteen-year-old believer, was arrested while attending a worship service. After brutal beatings he died in police custody, his hands and feet in chains. China Harvest says they have the names of one hundred evangelists currently in prison for preaching the gospel.

In this harsh climate, God seems especially pleased to honor His Word. In the late 1980s, Isaac Kim took one Bible to a village in northeast China. When he returned a few years later, there were ten thousand converts—all saying it was because of that one Bible he had brought.[5]

Many of China's officials are phobic, believing that a strong Christian presence has the power to topple communism.

They fear the collapse of communism as seen in eastern Europe and the old Soviet Union could be repeated there. According to a Puebla Program report, China's state-run press, in referring to Christianity, said, "If China does not want such a scene to be repeated in its land, it must strangle the baby while it is still in the manger."[6] (That must be one powerful Baby, who without any weapons can threaten a nuclear power and the government with the world's largest army!)

India is witnessing more violence against Christians than ever. I've been ministering in India for over twenty years. Only in the last few years have I sensed real danger. Until recently, historically pacifist Hinduism maintained a "live and let live" attitude. But the recent major inroads of Christianity have made this once-tolerant religion militant against Christians. No doubt Hindus feel threatened by the Indian church's impressive growth. In my discussions with India's missions strategists, some of them believe the Christian population of India now stands at 8 percent or even higher. Historically, for almost two thousand years the percentage of Christians in India has hovered around 2 or 3 percent. No wonder Hindus are upset! A single percentage point increase in India represents a huge number of people. But a six-percentage-point jump for the church in one decade—that's unprecedented!

Joseph D'Sousa, a church leader in India, believes there is " . . . a carefully orchestrated pattern to the violence propagated against Christians in India today. Fifteen documented attacks against Christian churches and missions took place in Gujarat state this summer . . . The violence is aimed at terrorizing the Indian Christian community and Christian involvement in all mission activity. It is against this backdrop that national missions continue to train, equip and mobilize national Christian workers to share the love of Christ . . . Over forty thousand nationals currently work in India full time. The future work for Christ in the nation will be built around the quiet work and prayers of nationals and not in great programs or meetings. Many factors will make big programs irrelevant and insensitive to the context in India."[7]

The Western church's investments and influence in India may be rapidly coming to an end. But a powerful indigenous church will remain.

What about persecution in the Western nations? Europe, of course, is no stranger to cruelty. The largest conflicts of the twentieth century's two world wars were played out on European soil. And the decade just past has witnessed unprecedented opportunities and major challenges for the church throughout Europe as walls literally came tumbling down. "We must renew the credibility of the Christian mission," notes Peter Kuzmic, president of the Evangelical Theological Seminary in Osijek, Yugoslavia. "Missions and evangelism are not primarily a question of methodology, money, management and numbers, but rather a question of authenticity, credibility and spiritual power . . . In going out to evangelize Yugoslavia, I frequently tell our seminary students that our main task may be simply to 'wash the face of Jesus,' for it has been dirtied and distorted by both the compromises of institutional Christianity through the centuries and the antagonistic propaganda of atheistic communism in recent decades."[8]

When Christians respond in a Christ-honoring way to persecution, they "wash the face of Jesus," displaying His beauty before an astounded world. And one new arena of persecution for Christians is—the United States.

THE DAY THAT CHANGED AMERICA

There's a silent revolution going on in America's high schools. Don't believe what you hear about a whole generation disinterested in the gospel. In the midst of a generation far from

God, there's a massive remnant comprised of some of the most sterling Christians to be found anywhere.

Little did Rachel Scott realize how far her love for Jesus would be felt. On May 2, 1998, Rachel wrote in her diary, "This will be my last year, Lord. I've gotten what I can. Thank you." Also recorded in what she thought would always be her private musings before the Lord, Rachel wrote, "I want heads to turn in the halls when I walk by. I want them to stare at me, watching and wanting the light you put in me. I want you to overflow my cup with your Spirit . . . I want you to use me to reach the unreached."[9]

God certainly answered Rachel's prayer. She had already signed up to go on a summer missions trip with Teen Mania. Rachel never took the trip—she was gunned down for her faith in the Columbine massacre. But literally hundreds of teenagers signed up to go in Rachel's place.

Then there's the story of Cassie Bernall, the girl who when asked, "Do you believe in God?," was murdered when she said yes. Here's what *Time* reporter Nancy Gibbs had to say about Cassie:

We expect our martyrs to be etched in stained glass, not carrying a backpack and worrying about their weight and their finals . . . the tale of a girl lost to bad friends and drugs and witchcraft and all the dark places of teenage rebellion. Even a youth minister who had some experience turning poisoned kids around had little hope for her . . . Her parents were advised to take her out of school, get her away from her friends, let her go only to church and hope for a miracle.

Her friends would say the prayers were answered. Converted at a Christian summer camp, Cassie was soon working with inner-city

gang members, attending Bible study and wearing a WHAT WOULD JESUS DO?
bracelet . . . The day after she died, her brother
found a poem that suggested she was already
on her journey "to find out what it really
means to suffer and to die with Him." Her
mother was in the shower a few days later, says
a family friend, and received a message, so
clearly: "For this reason, Cassie was born."[10]

Her friends made a tribute sign for her that read: "Cassie—
Thank you for fulfilling the Master's Commission. Your
faithfulness has touched the world." Cassie "fulfilled the
Master's Commission"—and "touched the world." Rachel
"reached the unreached." Don't tell me that America's brave
teenage martyrs aren't somehow tied in the heart of God to
a colossal new missions explosion.

> # "I want heads to turn in the halls when I walk by. I want them to stare at me, watching and wanting the light you put in me."

What kind of generation is this? What produces this kind
of devotion—this kind of sacrifice—from a girl who was flirt-
ing with witchcraft just a year or two earlier? And how does
a seventeen-year-old who struggles with the loss of friends
because she's a Jesus girl suddenly don regal robes of hero-
ism and offer the ultimate gift?

Cassie's and Rachel's parents are fine people, but they
would be the first to tell you that, other than their prayers
for their daughters, they did nothing especially noteworthy.

Neither Cassie nor Rachel ever trained for martyrdom.

So how, on that horrific day, were they able to step forward with such courage and grace? How did complacent, carnal, codependent America produce kids like that?

No one doubts the amazing strength and selfless sacrifice of the World War II generation, those Tom Brokaw calls the greatest generation America ever produced. But with all due respect (and much is due them), Brokaw may be wrong. For, hidden behind the piercing and tattoos, behind the headlines of the dopers and the spotlights on the rage-filled rappers and self-absorbed princesses, there is another emerging generation. Hidden from our view in classrooms where they daily take the jeers of teachers and students, tucked away in upstairs bedrooms where they are carving out a private history with God, a generation is being fashioned, the likes of which we've never seen. God is constructing Missions' Greatest Generation.

Winkey Pratney has been encouraging missions-hearted young people for a long time, but he senses a special destiny on this generation of youth. "You are survivors of a siege against divine destiny," Pratney writes. "Hidden somewhere among you is a promised child who has escaped the dragon. Only this time, there's not just one, but many. And they will take the battle to the ends of the world."[11]

HIGH-RISK MISSIONS

To live courageously for Jesus in your own country is one thing. But to take Him and His message cross-culturally takes risk to a whole new level.

Risk in missions is accelerating. In fact, the risks of missionary life have literally become front-page news. *The Chicago Tribune*, April 28, 2001, ran a story on page 1 titled "Missionaries facing world of new perils." The report noted the following as part of the cost of Christian missions:

> The Southern Baptist Convention, which has 5,000 missionaries in 180 countries, reports it has lost 98 in 100 years. The Wycliffe community counts 9 missionary deaths . . . New Tribes Mission . . . lost two missionaries who were shot to death in 1994 by leftist rebels in Colombia. But it hasn't given up on finding three missionaries kidnaped a year earlier in Panama and later taken to Colombia . . . Within a year New Tribes lost contact with the captors . . . Sam James of the Southern Baptist International Mission Board observed, "We have the same burning zeal and desire for people to know Jesus. It's a life-or-death commitment to the Lord."[12]

Satanic cults have sent members on assignment to kill all Protestant pastors in Cali, Colombia. Randy and Marcy MacMillian, along with their children, have literally learned to keep in step with the Spirit as a matter of life and death. Marcy notes the necessity of "keeping in fine tuning with the Holy Spirit to know what to do and what not to do." And according to Randy, such simple decisions as when to walk out the front door have become a matter of prayer.[13]

God is constructing Missions' Greatest Generation.

In the midst of growing hostility, it's important for us to realize why the heat against us is being turned up: We're being resisted because we're progressing. Jesus wasn't crucified because He was weak; He was crucified because He was strong and a threat to the status quo. In the same way, the church today is under siege, not because it is weak but because it is strong. And, where it is not being resisted, one has to wonder if it is because the light is dim and the salt has

191

lost its savor. After all, Scripture promises that "all who desire to live godly in Christ Jesus *will* suffer persecution" (2 Tim. 3:12, emphasis added).

If we have a firm grasp on the future, we can endure any hardship in the present.

Also, we need to remember that in Christ's kingdom the self-protective are actually those most at risk. Jesus warned, "For whoever desires to save his life will lose it, but whoever loses his life for My sake and the gospel's will save it" (Mark 8:35).

TAMING OUR RHETORIC

As the heat rises against Christians, we need to be reminded again that people are not the enemy. We cannot escape the scandal of the cross, nor do we wish to. Nevertheless, we are called to be gracious to those who oppose us. We are to be winsome in our witness. Jesus inferred that a key to evangelistic effectiveness is our winsomeness. "He who receives whomever I send," Jesus said, "receives Me" (John 13:20).

We will be better received if we learn to tame some of the rhetoric of our militant missions talk. This will prove helpful in prolonging our ministries. More importantly, it will help lower the defenses of those who oppose us and foster greater understanding.

Recently, an important Consultation on Mission Language and Metaphors convened at Fuller Seminary. The statement that grew out of the consultation includes the following admission:

We regret that certain words and images long
employed to call the church to mission have
increasingly caused offense to the very people

with whom we are seeking to share the Good
News. Some of these words and images are
biblical; some are motivational words from
the secular arena that we use to inspire
involvement and action. Many are military in
nature: "target," "conquer," "army,"
"crusade," "mobilize," "beachhead,"
"advance," "enemy," "battle."[14]

But there's an inherent challenge. I've used some of these
very words in this book, not to be provocative but because
they remain simply the best words to describe and define
missions initiatives. However, all of us in missions should
ask God for wisdom, sensitivity and prudence to use these
words judiciously. The Summary Statement of the
Consultation on Mission Language and Metaphors goes on
to encourage new strategies and motivations for missions:

As a motivation for missions involvement, people are responding to the call to glorify God
among the nations and wherever He is not yet
being worshiped. They also respond to the call
to follow Christ into servanthood and sacrifice,
the call to lift up the downtrodden, the call to a
life of great purpose and meaning in community with others of like mind. These are themes
around which we need to develop metaphors to
summon God's people to God's mission.

We need to remember that the code words we use in the
community of Christian believers often carry a very different
connotation among unbelievers. There may have been a time
when it was assumed that Christian publications would be read
almost exclusively by a Christian audience. With the Internet,
all that has changed. We need to assume that anything we pub-
lish will be read by antagonists as well as those who agree with

us. We know that radicals from other religions daily scour Christian websites looking for indicting rhetoric. Although I've written this book to Christians—and even to a sub-group among Christians—I assume this book will come into the hands of both missions enthusiasts and those who adamantly

Once again, we are a church of miracles, martyrdom, massive growth.

oppose Christian missions. I agree with the Consultation's supposition that "the new dynamics of globalization and instant global electronic information technologies are rapidly changing the context of our communication . . . The world, we must assume, will read or hear whatever we say to our own."

While I am completely convinced that Jesus and only Jesus is the sole hope of forgiveness and salvation, this belief does not give me *carte blanche* to disrespect the beliefs of others. On the contrary, my total confidence in the uniqueness of Jesus and the gospel frees me to interact with love and courtesy toward all people no matter what they believe. I concur with the spirit of The Amsterdam Declaration on this point:

The only way to know God in peace, love and joy is through the reconciling death of Jesus Christ, the risen Lord. As we share this message with others, we must do so with love and humility, shunning all arrogance, hostility and disrespect. As we enter into dialogue with adherents of other religions, we must be courteous and kind. But such dialogue must not be a substitute for proclamation. Yet because all persons are made in the image of God, we must advocate religious liberty and human rights for all. We pledge ourselves to treat those of other faiths with respect and faithfully and humbly serve the nation in which God has placed us, while affirming that Christ is the one and only Savior of the world.

ALIGNING WITH THE PERSECUTED CHURCH

At Amsterdam 2000, Luis Bush described what completing the Great Commission would look like. Bush said that essentially it would be "Jesus Christ, incarnate in His Body the church, reaching society at every level." In an evangelized world, the gospel would be in ascendance, and men and women from every people would gladly worship Him as their Lord.

It is this hope that presses us toward areas that to us are not "closed"; rather, they are "creatively open." If we have a firm grasp on the future, we can endure any hardship in the present. Jesus endured the pain of the cross "for the joy that was set before Him" (Heb. 12:2). The joy He foresaw was adoring worshipers from every tribe and nation. As we sow the seed of God's Word, we sow with absolute confidence. "My word...shall not return to Me void, but it shall accomplish what I please, and it shall prosper in the thing for which I sent it" (Isa. 55:11).

What an honor it is for me to meet with hidden heroes of the church from many nations, true heroes of the faith "of whom the world [is] not worthy" (Heb. 11:38). I think of Silas, a pastor from Sierra Leone who is living in a refugee camp. As he shared the story of his displacement with me, my heart went out to him. Seeing my response to his condition, he shook his head and smiled.

"Don't feel sorry for us," he told me. "We are not victims. God has placed us in Guinea to preach the gospel, especially to the Muslims." He is one of heaven's heroes, and totally unconscious of his status. As Silas perceives things, he is a servant of Christ and the gospel, no matter what his circumstances.

God-honoring passion is not just living dangerously, it's *loving* dangerously.

The Bible tells us to speak in behalf of those who have no voice. It is right and righteous for Christians to speak out against *all* oppression, whether the persecution is against us or against non-Christians. Granted, in our own nation, evangelicals seem to be targeted in a singularly unfair manner by those who vociferously support the rights of anyone and everyone else. Nevertheless, we dare not get on a defensive crusade for our own rights only. We must stand for human rights for all. And while we defend the "inalienable rights" of all, ultimately we submit to whatever conditions are most conducive for the gospel's advance—not because we are acquiescing to injustice, but because we see a greater cause than our own justice. In the words of The Millennial Manifesto:

We acknowledge that persecution and suffering are not only part of the Christian life, but also an opportunity for bold witness to the gospel in the power of the Spirit. We affirm the right of the church to proclaim the gospel in word and deed to everyone everywhere. We reject all forms of coercive proselytism and manipulative pressure, but uphold the right of persons to become followers of Jesus in response to the conviction of the Holy Spirit. We covenant together to endure persecution and hardship for the sake of the gospel, to

support prayerfully and defend persecuted
Christians, and to use every opportunity to
relieve their sufferings.

It is in the context of being a witness for Christ that Peter
encourages us: "Beloved, do not think it is strange concerning the fiery trial which is to try you, as though some strange
thing happened to to you; but rejoice to the extent that you
partake of Christ's sufferings, that when His glory is revealed,
you may also be glad with exceeding joy. If you are
reproached for the name of Christ, blessed are you, for the
Spirit of glory and of God rests upon you" (1 Pet. 4:12–14).

Just as it was in the church's beginning, so it is now as we
race toward the end of church age: Once again, we are a
church of miracles, martyrdom, massive growth. The church
father Tertullian is well known for his assertion that "the
blood of the martyrs is the seed of the church." That powerful statement was set in the context of an even bolder statement from this early church leader to secular authorities in
the second century:

Your cruelty does not profit you, however
exquisite. Instead, it tempts people to our sect.
As often as you mow us down, the more we
grow in number. The blood of the martyrs is
the seed of the church . . . We have filled all
you have—cities, islands, forts, towns, assembly
halls, even military camps, tribes, town
councils, the palace, senate, and forum. We
have left you nothing but the temples.[15]

THEIR BLOOD CRIES

God-honoring passion is not just living dangerously, it's *loving*
dangerously. And that love for the Lord and the lost has led
many to pay the ultimate price for the gospel's global advance.

At the headquarters of Living Word Missions in Tulsa, the magnificent "Hall of the Martyrs" tour is a powerful reminder of the cost of world evangelization. According to missions statistician David Barrett, one in every two hundred Christians living today can expect to be martyred. "Martyrdom has been a standard accompaniment of Christian mission because Christians inevitably arouse hostilities, and they pay the price," says Barrett.[16] This ultimate gift to Jesus remains, in Ed Silvoso's words, "a possibility on standby" for every follower of Christ.

If *tears* are precious to God, how much more precious must be the blood of the martyrs.

The possibility turned to reality for twenty-three-year-old Kim Jones. Two days before she died in the shooting at a midweek youth meeting at Wedgwood Baptist Church in Fort Worth, Texas, she wrote in her diary, "I don't ever want to lose the passion of being TOTALLY in love with you and you alone. God, please continue to stir my heart and make me passionate for you now and always!"[17]

Kim's prayer was answered. On that terrible night, September 15, 1999, seven people were killed and dozens more were injured before the assassin turned the gun on himself.

By the time Dr. Al Meredith, the church's pastor, became aware of the unfolding tragedy, he was catapulted into a new arena of visibility. In a few minutes' time, Dr. Meredith was launched from being a local church pastor to being an international spokesman for Christianity under fire. "In a sense, I prepared my whole life for that night," said Dr. Meredith. "The truths that are the foundations of my life just kicked in. All that I was raised with came forward."[18]

Siege on the Saints

Those foundational truths are now kicking in for many Christians around the world. Since the midnineties, thousands of North Korean Christians have been martyred, many by communist firing squads. Since 1953, twenty-three hundred churches in North Korea with some three hundred thousand members have disappeared. Christian informers say that at least four thousand Christians have been executed since 1999 for the "crime" of possessing a Bible. And in the last few years, at least three thousand Christians have died in the violence in Indonesia.

Added to these are the stories and statistics we will never hear. They are, nevertheless, recorded. The Bible says that God keeps a record of our tears (Ps. 56:8). If *tears* are precious to God, how much more precious must be the blood of the martyrs. Further, Scripture says that those who reverence the Lord are recorded in a book of remembrance (Mal. 3:16). Surely there is a special section of that book reserved for those who honor Him with their very lives.

At the end of time, John saw an awesome scene where the martyrs' blood was eloquently appealing to God: "I saw under the altar the souls of those who had been slain for the word of God and for the testimony which they held. And they cried with a loud voice, saying, 'How long, O Lord, holy and true, until You judge and avenge our blood on those who dwell on the earth?'" (Rev. 6:9–10).

Shouldn't we add our voices to the throng of slain witnesses? "How long, O Lord? How long before their sacrifice is rewarded? How long until Your glory fills the earth? May the Lamb receive the reward of *His* sacrifice! When this happens, Your martyrs will receive the reward for *their* sacrifices."

Not long ago I met Mincaye, a member of the spear-wielding Huaorani killing party who massacred Jim Elliot, Nate Saint and three other gallant missionaries in 1955. Today, Steve Saint, Nate's son, lives with his family among the Huaorani. Mincaye is now an elder in the Huaorani church. And the man who killed Steve's dad is now referred to as *grandfather* by Steve's children.

You can counter aggression with reprisals. You can counter rhetoric with rhetoric. You can counter bombs with bombs. But aggressive love— how do you counter *that?*

Only the grace of God can accomplish that. Before thousands of evangelists at Amsterdam 2000, Mincaye gave this testimony:

When I killed Steve's father, I didn't know better. No one told us that he had come to show us God's trail. My heart was black and sick in sin, but I heard [that] God sent His own Son, His blood dripping and dripping. He washed my heart clean ... Now I see you God-followers from all over [the world]. I see well my brothers and sisters that God's blood has washed your hearts, too. Go speak [about God] all over the world. Let's take many with us to God's place in heaven.

Just recently has the full story been revealed that the five missionaries had loaded weapons with them—guns that, in that moment of horror and glory, they chose not to use.

You can counter aggression with reprisals. You can counter rhetoric with rhetoric. You can counter bombs with bombs. But aggressive love—how do you counter *that?* No wonder Scripture urges us, "Beloved, do not avenge yourselves, but rather give place to wrath; for it is written, 'Vengeance is Mine,

I will repay,' says the Lord. Therefore, 'If your enemy is hungry, feed him; if he is thirsty, give him a drink; for in so doing you will heap coals of fire on his head.' Do not be overcome by evil, but overcome evil with good" (Rom. 12:19–21).

Our secret weapon is supernatural love, a love that never fails, even when such love evokes brutal hostility. Where does this kind of love come from? "The love of God has been poured out in our hearts by the Holy Spirit who was given to us" (Rom. 5:5). As we respond with love toward our enemies, God responds with His favor on us. "You will arise and have mercy on Zion; for the time to favor her, yes, the set time, has come . . . So the nations shall fear the name of the LORD, and all the kings of the earth Your glory" (Ps. 102:13, 15).

STOP THIS!

With Isaiah, we can say, "Your name and renown are the desire of our hearts" (Isa. 26:8, NIV). And often, as we've seen in this chapter, His renown comes at a price.

Look at Paul's utter abandon to Jesus: "If we live, we live to the Lord; and if we die, we die to the Lord. Therefore, whether we live or die, we are the Lord's" (Rom. 14:8). Don't you feel Paul's longing behind those words for the renown of His name? It's just hard to intimidate a man like that. Paul preached Christ across a hostile, pluralistic empire with immaculate disinterest in the consequences to him. When he was imprisoned on trumped-up charges, Roman authorities and Jewish religious leaders thought they had finally silenced this trouble maker and that things would "get back to normal." But Paul knew that the seed of the gospel is incorruptible and that what he had set in motion was irreversible. Pagan Rome would topple; the gospel would prevail. As Winkey Pratney wryly observed, "Nero finally caught Paul, put him in prison and cut off his head. Now we call our dogs 'Nero' and our sons 'Paul.'"[19]

Like Paul, Telemachus was abandoned to Jesus. A second-century monk with an intense love for Christ, as a Christian he respected the innate dignity of all people. Thus, he couldn't believe the cruelty of the gladiator matches he had heard about, especially in "civilized" Rome. On a trip to Rome, he decided to see for himself. Entering the great coliseum, he watched in unbelieving shock as the gladiators hacked each other to death before the cheering, bloodthirsty crowd. Finally, his redeemed sensitivities could take no more. Telemachus jumped into the arena himself. He wedged his body between the dueling gladiators and yelled, "In the name of Jesus Christ, stop this!"

The seed of the gospel will take root, and the Seed of David will rule.

At first the crowd was stunned. Then they turned their blood lust on him. Hundreds of men stormed the arena, beating Telemachus to a bloody pulp and finally killing him.

Suddenly a hush swept over the coliseum. The emperor, who moments before had given his crazed endorsement to the state-sponsored gladiator killings, stood in mortified silence and then left in disgust. Slowly, the subdued crowd, brought to their senses by the bold submission of Telemachus, exited the coliseum.

That was the last gladiator match in Rome. Though the Roman "civilization" was dying, one Christian's righteous outrage had awakened true civility. And history would never be the same.

Today, also at great risk, the heirs of Telemachus are standing in the gap for a hell-bent world. Heartbroken over a world gone mad, they too are crying out, "In the name of Jesus Christ, stop this!" And because of the gospel, at some point the insanity will stop. The seed of the gospel will take root, and the Seed of David will rule.

No matter how fierce the resistance, the finish line is in sight. Those who oppose us may slow our progress, but they cannot keep us from the goal. They cannot prevent the inevitable—Jesus will be known, adored and lavishly worshiped by every tribe, people and nation. I am a firm believer in the ultimate triumph of truth.

Though the cause of evil prosper,
Yet the truth alone is strong;
Though her portion be the scaffold,
And upon the throne be wrong,
Yet that scaffold sways the future,
And, behind the dim unknown,
Stands our God within the shadow
Keeping watch above His own.[20]

We are all, at heart, gradualists, our expectations set by the steady passage of time. But the world of the Tipping Point is a place where the unexpected becomes expected, where radical change is more than possibility. It is—contrary to all our expectations—a certainty.
—MALCOLM GLADWELL

Let us light a fire of commitment to proclaim the gospel of Jesus Christ in the power of the Holy Spirit to the ends of the earth, using every resource at our command and with every ounce of our strength.
—BILLY GRAHAM
AUGUST 6, 2000

This is our faith tremendous,
Our wild hope who shall scorn?
That in the name of Jesus
The earth shall be reborn.
—VACHEL LINDSAY

TEN

Finish Line in Sight!

"For from the rising of the sun, even to its going down, My name shall be great among the Gentiles; in every place incense shall be offered to My name, and a pure offering; for My name shall be great among the nations," says the LORD of hosts.
—MALACHI 1:11

You are worthy to take the scroll, and to open its seals; for You were slain, and have redeemed us to God by Your blood out of every tribe and tongue and people and nation.
—REVELATION 5:9

Are you here to make a political statement?"

As I walked backstage, the tape recorders clicked on, and the reporters' pads and pens were ready. I was speaking at an interdenominational prayer rally in a Midwestern city. Somehow the press of that city perceived this rally as a politically tainted event. It was not; we gathered merely as Christians across denominations to pray for harvest and revival. Nevertheless, when I arrived at the rally site, the press were there to meet me. "Have you come here to make a political statement?" they asked again, shoving microphones in my face.

"Yes, I have," I responded. "Are you ready?" I smiled. "Here's my political statement: *The kingdoms of this world will become the kingdoms of our Lord and of His Christ, and He will reign forever and ever!*[1] That's where I stand—that's my political statement!"

Administrations come and go. Empires come and go. But God's kingdom is forever, and He has given you the high dignity of helping move history toward His unrivaled reign.

THREE FUTURE EVENTS

The Scottish writer Thomas Carlyle observed, "He who has no vision of eternity will never get a true hold of time." The best time management technique I know is to live in light of eternity.

There are three future events that help frame what we do with this vapor called time. They will happen as surely as tomorrow's sunrise.

THE GREAT WHITE THRONE JUDGMENT

John describes the first event in Revelation 20:

> Then I saw a great white throne and Him who sat on it, from whose face the earth and the heaven fled away. And there was found no place for them. And I saw the dead, small and great, standing before God, and the books were opened. And another book was opened, which is the Book of Life . . . And anyone not found written in the Book of Life was cast into the lake of fire.
>
> —REVELATION 20:11-12, 15

The Great White Throne Judgment is the judgment of unbelievers, those whose names are not in the Book of Life. We should be forever grateful that we have escaped this awesome judgment because we have placed our faith in Christ. When we are born again, our names are placed in the Book of Life. But what about the rest of humanity?

Finish Line in Sight!

This sure day of judgment spurs me to *evangelism*.

THE JUDGMENT SEAT OF CHRIST

Paul describes the second event in 2 Corinthians 5:10–11:

**For we must all appear before the judgment seat
of Christ, that each one may receive the things
done in the body, according to what he has
done, whether good or bad. Knowing, therefore, the terror of the Lord, we persuade men.**

The Judgment Seat of Christ is the judgment of believers,
when our whole postconversion life will come up for review.
The greatest tragedy would be to miss heaven altogether. The
second greatest tragedy would be to go into heaven empty-
handed, with no rewards to lay at the pierced feet of Jesus in
gratitude for His gift of salvation. The Judgment Seat of
Christ motivates me to *holiness*.

THE COMPANY OF THE REDEEMED

The final great event is described by John in Revelation
chapters 5 and 7. He sees a company of the redeemed of all
ages who are lavishly worshiping God.

**After these things I looked, and behold, a great
multitude which no one could number, of all
nations, tribes, peoples, and tongues, standing
before the throne and before the Lamb,
clothed with white robes, with palm branches
in their hands, and crying out with a loud
voice, saying, "Salvation belongs to our God
who sits on the throne, and to the Lamb!"**
—REVELATION 7:9

This is mission accomplished! God's covenant promise to
Abraham to bring blessing to every culture and people is now
fulfilled. (See Genesis 12:3.) There are representative
redeemed men and women from *"all* nations, tribes, peoples

and languages!" This thrilling event impels me to *missions* and to throw my life and energies into the battle to bring closure on the Great Commission.

This is why I am hooked with the missions addiction! Living in light of these three great events enables you to live with focus, joy and worship. It helps you trash the trivia and live with a sense of both urgency and assurance.

POSTMILLENNIAL DEPRESSION

But some have lost the urgency because of discouragement and fatigue. As one former missions addict told me, "Radicalism is tiring." Many in missions today are teetering between optimism and despair. There had been great hope that by the beginning of this new millennium we might actually see closure on the Great Commission. "A church for every people and the gospel for every person by A.D. 2000" was our watchword. But by the midnineties, it was apparent that the vision of getting the gospel to every person by December 31, 2000 would not be realized.

"Preach the gospel by all means. If necessary, use words."

We then modified the vision to "a church for every people" by A.D. 2000 as a base from which the gospel could then go to every person. But this goal too was not met.

Where then does that leave us as we begin the inaugural decade of this new millennium? Frankly, it has left some encouraged, many exhausted and even more confused. It is time to revisit the Great Commission once again and recall exactly what our Lord told us to do.

He told us to *evangelize every person on the planet.* That is the literal translation of Mark 16:15: "Go into all the world and preach the gospel to every person." Notice the inclusive nature of this commission: *All believers* are to proclaim the Good News as they go, and they are to preach it in *all the world* to *all people.* No believer is exempted from sharing, and no unbeliever is to be excluded from hearing.

We proclaim the gospel in many ways. Jesus said, "Let your light so shine before men, that they may see your good works and glorify your Father in heaven" (Matt. 5:16). I love Francis Xavier's adage, "Preach the gospel by all means. If necessary, use words."

Jesus also commanded us to *make disciples of every people group.* "Go therefore and make disciples of all the nations" (Matt. 28:19). The word translated "nations" is *ethne* in the original language–a Greek word we have transliterated as *ethnic groups.* Jesus was clearly saying that every ethno-linguistic people group was to be turned from darkness into disciples, from those who oppose Him to those who worship Him.

The first part of the commission–preaching the gospel to every person–is doable in our lifetime. We have enough money to do it, *if* we will allocate it. We have the human resources, *if* we will deploy them. The greater issue, greater than the need for money or manpower, is *if* we have the will.

Once the gospel is preached and received–at least by some–among every tribe, people and language, then comes the equally great assignment of turning Christ's enemies into His followers. This is the task of disciple making, the challenge of discipling the nations.

Evangelizing every person will require renewed urgency and passion. Discipling every people will require tenacity and endurance. Sprinters develop explosive speed; marathon runners develop pain-denying endurance. What is the need for our day? Both! Youth can provide the speed, and elders can provide the endurance. Stan Guthrie warns:

**The danger is that many who have been sprint-
ing toward the finish line may give up with the**

realization that they are in a grueling
marathon. Such disobedience, however, would
not only belittle Christ, who bought our
salvation on the cross, but also mock the
bravery of all who have gone before us in
centuries past to share the gospel.[2]

There is much ground yet to be taken, many peoples yet to be reached, many nations yet to be discipled. But God is calling out "eleventh hour workers" into His harvest. Since Jesus' time we have not had adequate workers commensurate to the size of this harvest. "The harvest truly is plentiful, but the laborers are few" (Matt. 9:37). But the harvests are so abundant now that they are piling on top of each other! "'Behold, the days are coming,' says the LORD, 'when the plowman shall overtake the reaper'" (Amos 9:13). God is calling out "eleventh-hour workers" to reap this unprecedented harvest. (See Matthew 20:6–7.) You may be one of them.

Our disappointments that we have not finished the job sooner need to be marinated in the juices of biblical hope. And there is plenty of hope when it comes finishing the task. Some generation is going to grab hold of this. Some generation will be so hooked by the missions addiction that the Great Commission will become the *great completion!*

GREAT COMMISSION TIPPING POINT

With all my heart I believe we are that chosen generation! More than any previous generation we can claim the magnificent promise, "But you are a chosen generation, a royal priesthood, a holy nation, His own special people, that you may proclaim the praises of Him who called you out of darkness into His marvelous light" (1 Pet. 2:9).

I can sense it. Something is going to happen in this decade—a Great Commission *tipping point.* Author Malcolm Gladwell describes a "tipping point" as "the moment of critical mass, the threshold, the boiling point."[3] It is a "point of no return" that makes the desired outcome inevitable.

An excellent example from history is D-Day in World War II. After the invasion of Normandy, a beachhead was established that made eventual victory for the Allies not just plausible, but unpreventable. With a sufficient presence and beachhead on enemy territory, although many more lives would be required before the war was officially over, the victory was irrevocably certain.

Some generation will be so hooked by the missions addiction that the Great Commission will become the *great completion!*

I am absolutely convinced that in this inaugural decade of the third millennium we will experience the equivalent of a Great Commission D-Day. There will be a tipping point in the Spirit that will bring entire nations under the sway of the gospel in record time.

Often natural events announce imminent parallel spiritual realities. For instance, the tearing down of the Berlin Wall was a leading spiritual indicator that the walls of communism were coming down and that all the Balkans and the former Soviet Union would be open to the gospel. It was a domino effect—it happened fast and unexpectedly.

Today, we see the same phenomenon. There are more "new" geopolitical nations that have been birthed in the last decade than in any previous ten-year period. This foreshadows an impending spiritual reality of rapid spiritual birth for entire people groups as they will be swept into covenant relationship with the one true God through the gospel.

Who has ever heard such a thing?
Who has ever seen such things?
Shall the earth be made to give birth in one day?
Or shall a nation be born at once?
For as soon as Zion was in labor,
She gave birth to her children.
—Isaiah 66:8 [4]

Nations (i.e. peoples) will literally be born spiritually in a day.

Almost everyone who reads the previous paragraph will question whether entire peoples can turn to Christ in a single day of glorious evangelistic triumph. But *someone* will read it with prophetic discernment, biblical hope and God-honoring faith. I pray that someone is you.

I am absolutely convinced that in this inaugural decade of the third millennium we will experience the equivalent of a Great Commission D-Day.

Scripture is replete with promises of the ultimate reign of Jesus among every people. He will get the glory due His name expressed through the unique beauty of every culture and every people. Paul skims some of the highlights of these promises in Romans 15, quoting from passages in Deuteronomy, 2 Samuel, Psalms and Isaiah that confirm the unswerving commitment of God to enthrone His Messiah over every people. Then—in the midst of these assurances of Christ's ultimate victory—Paul issues one of the most thrilling benedictions in the entire Bible:

Now may the God of hope fill you with all joy
and peace in believing, that you may abound

in hope by the power of the Holy Spirit.
—ROMANS 15:13

May the God of hope fill you with confident faith . . . faith for what? Faith to believe the promises just quoted! Faith to believe genuinely that Jesus shall reign over *every* people, language and nation!

In *The Pilgrim's Progress,* Christian encounters a dark, ominous region on his way to the Celestial City. He realizes his vision has been darkened by the chilling shadows from Doubting Castle. Fighting despair, he calls on the inner resources of a faith in God's promises. With John Bunyan's pilgrim, we too have "a key in our bosom called promise."

Do you *really believe* that God will write the last chapter and ensure that His Son receives loving worship from every tribe and nation? To doubt this sure promise is to exchange the triumphant Son for a caricature. "The reason some of us are such poor specimens of Christianity," says Oswald Chambers, "is because we have no almighty Christ. We have Christian attributes and experiences, but there is no abandonment to Jesus . . . Beware of the satisfaction of sinking back and saying—'It can't be done'; you know it can be done if you look to Jesus."[5]

World evangelization? *Every* tribe and nation? It can be done! Why? Because we have an almighty Christ.

WELCOMING THE WONDERS

God is clearly at work in dramatic ways around the world and going to great lengths to show His power and love to every people.

When I was in the Pacific island nation of Fiji, I heard how God is using Bible college students as well as seasoned ministers to display His power. One Fijian student named Nina had gone to Papua New Guinea to do village evangelism. There she discovered a village almost totally under the control of demons. She simply began to lay hands on the people, including the children, commanding evil spirits to leave in Jesus' name. Immediately people began to be healed of long-standing infirmities, and some who were deaf began to hear. An old man who just sat observing all of this determined that he would speak out against this move of God's Spirit. But as he began to speak, he fell from his chair and was unable to open his mouth. He repented and opened his heart to Christ. Another woman, who had drunk a concoction of beetle juice prepared by a witch doctor, had a choking lump in her throat ever since she drank the potion. But when she renounced the witchcraft and declared Jesus as her Lord, the lump immediately disappeared. These notable healings softened the hearts of the entire village toward the Lord, and many were swept into the kingdom of God. [6]

Now entire books are being written about present-day signs and wonders, including *Stories from the Front Lines: Power Evangelism in Today's World* by Jane Rumph (Chosen Books) and *The Move of the Holy Spirit in the 10/40 Window* by Luis Bush and Beverly Pegues (YWAM Publishing). Included are multiple accounts of healing, prophecies, dreams and visions, miracles and encounters with angels.

Evangelist Mike Francen says, "God is calling us to do things that have never been done in places that no one has ever dared try!" The late Bob Pierce, founder of World Vision and Samaritan's Purse, often referred to this as "God room." It is the arena of the supernatural extra, or, as he put it, "that space between what is possible and what He wants done that is impossible."

Kirk DeVenney, veteran missionary to Guatemala, told me a thrilling story of "God room" at work. In December 1999 he was driving a bus through Mexico, headed for Guatemala. It was loaded with thirty-five cases of Spanish Bibles, four thousand copies of God's Word. "At that time we really didn't need the Bibles for our work in Guatemala, but I just felt that I should take the Bibles with us." Kirk picks up the story:

My seventeen-year-old son and I crossed the border of the United States into Mexico on a Saturday afternoon and stayed that night in a small hotel about two hours south of the border. We rose very early on Sunday morning to begin our three-day drive back home to Guatemala. We had made this trip over twenty times in the last twelve years.

"God is calling us to do things that have never been done in places that no one has ever dared try!"

About six hours south into Mexico, the back shocks and springs on the bus broke. We found ourselves broken down in the town of Manual, Mexico, at 10:00 A.M. on a Sunday morning. The bus had broken down in front of a welder's shop. The welder told us that he did not have shocks or springs for our bus, but he would weld a piece of steel under the bus that would level it out and enable us to go on to Guatemala.

We had to unload all thirty-five cases of the Bibles from the bus. As we were unloading the heavy cases I mentioned to my son that if I knew someone to give the Bibles to, I would gladly do it. My son mentioned that he had just heard two men close to the welder's shop discussing something from the Bible. I ran to the location where my son said he had seen

215

the men, but they were gone. However, I did see a man about a hundred yards away. I ran to him and asked if he was a Christian. The man answered, "No, I am a Jehovah's Witness." I told him that I was looking for evangelical Christians. He responded, "Would a Pentecostal church be all right?"

I shouted, "Yes, that would be great!" We walked for about fifteen minutes through the back streets of Manual until he pointed me to the Assembly of God church. Inside a gray-haired pastor was teaching about fifteen people. I went inside and motioned to a man sitting in the back row to come outside with me.

The man slipped out of the building with me, and I told him what had happened to us and that I had four thousand Bibles that I wanted to donate to this church. He started jumping up and down and shouting, "We have our Bibles! We have our Bibles!"

Then the man ran to the platform, interrupted the pastor and told him what I had said. They both began jumping, praising God and shouting, "We have our Bibles! We have our Bibles!"

The service was over! Everyone present came out and told me that seven months earlier in a prayer meeting the Lord spoke to them as a church that they were to canvas every home in Manual between Christmas and the new year as a gift to Him for the new millennium. The Lord impressed them that they were to present the gospel to every home and *leave a new Bible at every home.* As a small church, they did not have the money to buy this many Bibles, but they were intent to some-how obey the word of the Lord.

One week earlier, before my "unscheduled stop" in Manual, there was a prophetic word that "a man will come to you and give you the Bibles." Then one week later I showed up on their doorstep with an offer of four thousand Bibles. How many homes are in Manual, Mexico? You guessed it: four thousand![7]

This thrilling story is but one example of the extraordinary lengths to which God will go to bring His love and light to needy people. Let us never forget that all of these wonders from God's hand are for a specific purpose—the advance of the

> ## It is time for "the whole church to take the whole gospel to the whole world."

gospel and making disciples of all nations. At Pentecost, Peter pointed the curious to Calvary. Demonstrations of power that become ends in themselves disconnect from the spirit of the gospel. If we emphasize Pentecostal potency without Calvary's cross, eventually we get power without love. And power with-out love always turns brutal. *Jesus* is our message.

When people get a grip on the gospel and the gospel gets a grip on them, they are lifted in every dimension—spiritually, physically and economically. But the message, the focus, the attraction is *Jesus*. The Lord reminded Abraham after He abundantly blessed him, "I am your shield, your exceedingly great reward" (Gen. 15:1). God was reminding Abraham that the greatest blessing of covenant is relationship with Him, not the benefits that relationship brings.

To reap today's unprecedented harvest, the great missions

need is more laborers. It is not God's intent merely to empower select individuals to flow in miracle anointing. God longs to empower His whole church! As the Lausanne Covenant states, it is time for "the whole church to take the whole gospel to the whole world." "*You* shall receive power when the Holy Spirit has come upon *you* . . ." (Acts 1:8, emphasis added). The power of the Holy Spirit verifies the gospel and enables us to be Christ's witnesses to the ends of the earth.

If anyone could have trusted in academic credentials or the strength of his reasoning skills, it was the apostle Paul. Yet Paul knew that there is a vast difference between winning arguments and winning hearts. Laying aside confidence in his considerable personal deftness, he wrote, "And my speech and my preaching were not with persuasive words of human wisdom, but in demonstration of the Spirit and of power, that your faith should not be in the wisdom of men but in the power of God" (1 Cor. 2:4–5).

JUST DO IT

Often Christians check out mentally and emotionally when they hear the "M" word—*missions*. They reason, "Well, I'm not called to be a missionary (at least I *hope* not!), so none of this missions stuff really applies to me."

All right, it's time to talk very seriously about just why God gave you the honor of being part of the first generation of Christians in this new millennium. It's true, not every believer is gifted as a cross-cultural missionary, but *every* Christian—I'm talking about *you*—is called to be a witness for Christ, and *every* Christian has a role to play in bringing international acclaim to His name. John Piper writes, "Not every Christian is called to be a missionary. But every follower of Christ is called to be a world Christian. A world Christian is someone who is so gripped by the glory of God and the glory of His global purpose that he chooses to align himself with God's mission to fill the earth with the knowledge of His glory . . . Everything a world Christian does he does with a view to the hallowing of God's name and the coming of God's kingdom among all the peoples of the earth."[8]

So there is a difference between being called to be a *missionary* and being called to *missions*. Not every believer has the missionary gift, but every Christian is called to some kind of involvement in missions. We are all called to advance the gospel in some way and to participate in the fulfilling of God's purposes in our generation. There is a role God wants you to play in helping to fulfill His purposes in this late hour of history. It is a role tailor-made for you, and only you can fill that particular role. How do you find where you fit in missions?

DISCOVER YOUR SPIRITUAL GIFTS.

God has only gifted children! He has given every believer certain spiritual gifts—and that includes you. These gifts are for edifying and building up the body of Christ. You may have the gift of administration. If so, consider utilizing that gift as a volunteer with a missions organization, or God may want to use you permanently in the administrative side of a missions ministry. If you have the gift of helps, pray about investing your vacation time in going and doing some of the hands-on labor that takes up so much of the time of missionaries and national pastors. If you have the gift of tongues, you can move into intercession and prophetic worship in an even deeper way for the nations and unreached peoples of the world.

DEVELOP YOUR NATURAL ABILITIES.

Natural abilities are not the same as spiritual gifts, although they usually complement each other. You can utilize your natural abilities for the advance of the gospel. Has God given you the ability to sing or to compose music? Use that talent in any opening God gives you, including nursing homes and inner-city missions. Participating in ministries like these brings God's smile on your life. Are you a mechanic? Believe me, you are needed in missions, and you can bring great blessing and help to many missionaries.

Also, you can just look for ways to be a blessing. Once in

If you are not taking advantage of opportunities to share your faith where you are right now, it is very unlikely that an airplane ticket and a visa to another country will automatically transform you into an effective witness.

the Philippines, I gave two hundred dollars to a missionary couple who were working in a remote area. I told them, "This is a designated gift. I want you to go to a nice hotel, have a nice dinner and take a break tonight." The next morning I had breakfast with this couple. With tears in her eyes, the wife told me, "You will never know how refreshing it was just to sleep in air conditioning last night."

DEFINE YOUR CIRCUMSTANCES.

If you are careful and sacrificial as a steward, you will probably have at least some discretionary money. Use it to advance the gospel around the world. If family obligations prevent you from going physically, remember that your light can shine wherever you are and that there are plenty of cross-cultural opportunities for ministry right in your own home town.

A young man once said to me, "I'm called to Germany."

Only half teasing, I smiled and said, "No, you're not."

"What do you mean?" he retorted.

"My point is, you're not called to Germany; you're called to *Germans*, and before you uproot your family and move to Germany, I'd like to know about your ministry right here in this city to those people whose primary language and culture are German."

DISCERN THE SEASONS OF LIFE.

Many excellent missionaries serving today are in a second career. God may be calling you to hands-on missionary service later. While there is not a definitive rule for every family, unless your children are small or grown, you are probably not in a season conducive to uprooting your family to another culture. But wherever God puts you, discern what season of life He has placed you in, and live to bring Him glory in every season of life.

A wise college professor taught me this principle: *As now, so then.* In other words, if you are not taking advantage of opportunities to share your faith where you are right now, it is very unlikely that an airplane ticket and a visa to another country will automatically transform you into an effective witness. If you haven't laid the proper spiritual foundations of a daily, growing relationship with God, there's little hope that a change of climate and culture (where you will have less free time and more open hostility) will deepen your walk with the Lord.

There is a role God wants you to play in helping to bring Him global glory. It is a role tailor-made for you, and only you can fill that role. How do you find where you fit in God's big plan?

Your most important step in contracting the missions addiction is to prayerfully examine your role in today's harvest. You can be a *go-er*, a *pray-er*, a *giver*, an *encourager*, a *welcomer* and an *advocate*.

Put before God the possibility that He wants you to be a *go-er*—part of the church's international missionary force for century 21. God calls some as career missionaries to devote the major portion of their lives to cross-cultural, hands-on missionary service. Perhaps He wants you to give a significant slice of your future to Him as a short-term missionary. Or perhaps you should just start by being part of a team missions outreach from your church or a credible missions organization.

If you feel prompted by the Spirit to go, with wise counsel, start preparing now. A seasoned missionary once told me how God launched his hopes into reality. "As long as I was willing to go but in my heart I was planning to stay, nothing happened," he told me. "But when I even surrendered the vision and said, 'Lord, I'm willing to stay, but as of today I'm going to start planning to go,' that's when things really began to pop."

You can play a significant role in global harvest this very day as a *pray-er*. There are excellent resources available to help you pray intelligently and systematically for every nation and unreached people group. Also, pray for missionaries and national pastoral leaders you know by name. Don't forget to pray over current events, asking the Holy Spirit to engineer the circumstances among every people and nation to draw them to Christ. Weave the threefold cord referred to in chapter five of global intercession, spiritual warfare and prophetic worship.

Begin now to be a *giver*. You should give directly above the tithe to your church for the advance of the gospel. Give to your church's missions outreaches, to missionary families and to worthy missions ministries. Many Christians are now earmarking at least 1 percent of their income directly to penetrate the remaining peoples and plant churches among them.

There are tremendous opportunities, not far from where you live, to be a *welcomer*. One of the most fruitful arenas of evangelism today is through befriending international students. These students are often brilliant, affluent and influential, the future leaders of their nations. The repercussions of loving ministry to them are enormous!

Above all, be an *encourager*. Look for opportunities to give a word of encouragement to missionaries, indigenous leaders and all who are involved in spreading the gospel. Just think what one phone call or e-mail today could mean to weary soldiers of the cross on the frontlines.

Finally, consider becoming a missions *advocate*. Offer to serve on your church's missions committee. Volunteer to help in missions conferences. Become the most knowledgeable person you can be in missions. And when it comes time for your influence to make a difference, be an advocate for the world's economically and spiritually destitute. Don't miss any chance to impact others. Let's always remember that the dark side of missions history is the tragedy of missed opportunities. So look for ways to inject others with the missions addiction!

Don't just sit there waiting for God to overwhelm you. You are *already* under His commission. You may have a major encounter, as did Isaiah, Saul and John. But probably you will sense a still, small voice. Take the counsel of those who have gone before you: "From the stories of others who have become involved in missions work, we learn that the initial inner urgings often seem very subtle, hard to discern. In fact, for most of us, the message really doesn't become clear until we act. It is the process of taking action in response to the Holy Spirit's urging that often provides the real clarity. Without responding, you'll probably never know."[9]

The master key to finding your place in God's big plan is to act on every prompting of the Holy Spirit. In missions, relationships breed more relationships, and obeyed opportunities breed more opportunities. There are two ways to learn to swim: Step-by-step instruction in the shallow end or the rather more dramatic "crash course" of *diving into the deep end!* Either way, just overcome inertia and *begin*.

AN ANOINTING OF SPEED

If it is not this generation of Christians—we who have seen God's gracious renewal, we who possess more data on global harvest than any previous generation, we who stand on the shoulders of twenty centuries of missionary giants—if it is not us God wants to fulfill the Great Commission, then *who else is it?*

And if we are not to throw all our hearts and energies into the global harvest now—as the Spirit sweeps over the nations, now that we have actually targeted every unreached people, now as eschatological hopes loom large at the beginning of this new millennium—then *when* will there be a more opportune time?

I am not suggesting that we run off in all directions with mere human enthusiasm that is fueled by a noble cause. I *am* urging that we be imbued with the spirit of the sons of Issachar who understood the times and knew what the people of God should do. (See 1 Chronicles 12:32.) May we too have an understanding of our times and a clear discernment of what these times demand. This is no time to be idle. It is a time to work tirelessly—in the Spirit's strength, in the Father's ripe vineyard, for the honor of the Son. We must always remember that harvest is seasonal. Urgency presses us on. Jesus said, "I must work the works of Him who sent Me while it is day; the night is coming when no one can work" (John 9:4).

God believes in you! He believes in you so much He has given you the prime slot in the race; you have the honor of being a last lap runner!

When I was about eight years old, our gym coach picked four of us boys to run a relay race. He looked at me first and said, "David, you're not very fast, so you run first." (That's always "encouraging" to a little boy!) Then he said to the others, "Brian, you're a little faster, so you run second. Brad, you're even faster, so you run the third lap. And John, you're the fastest of all; you get to run last! You are the one who can actually win the race! When you get the baton, don't worry whether you're ahead or behind. Don't be distracted by anything around you; just fix your eyes on the finish line and run with all the speed you have!"

There are two ways to learn to swim: Step-by-step instruction in the shallow end or the rather more dramatic "crash course" of *diving into the deep end!* Either way, just overcome inertia and *begin.*

In the very same way, God has honored you with the prime slot in the race; you are a last lap runner! You have been chosen for history's highest assignment—to finally fulfill Christ's mandate to get the gospel to every person and make disciples of every people!

TAKE THIS POSITION

Don't "couch-potato" your way through life, either ignorant of or indifferent to God's glory in the earth and His purpose for your times. As Ron Luce says, "Live God loud!" Don't be among the sad group whose biggest thrill is the next concert and whose finest skill is channel surfing. Suddenly they realize that the sand has sifted through the hourglass. They are out of time, out of touch and, if they do go to heaven, out of treasure. They have accomplished the sum total of nothing of eternal value.

Nate Saint, one of the five missionaries martyred in Ecuador in 1956, wrote, "People who don't know the Lord [and we might add Christians who just don't "get it"] ask why in the world we waste our lives as missionaries. They forget that they too are expending their lives, and when the bubble has burst they will have nothing of eternal significance to show for the years they have wasted."

God is calling you today to a higher life. I am asking Him to use this book to jolt thousands out of apathy and inject them with the missions addiction. Oswald Chambers wrote,

Whatever else you do, don't die inch by inch, playing little games. Live for what matters!

"God brings us to a point of climax. That is the Great Divide in the life; from that point we either go toward a more and more dilatory and useless type of Christian life, or we become more and more ablaze for the glory of God—my utmost for *His* highest."[10] This very moment could be your Great Divide.

In research for this book, I spent a day in the Yale Divinity School library in New Haven, Connecticut. There I perused the original papers of the Student Volunteer Movement and the missionary statesman John R. Mott. One hundred years ago Mott wrote an impassioned book titled *The Evangelization of the World in This Generation*. Before the book's publication, he sent manuscript copies to selected people asking for their comments and suggestions. One of those manuscripts went to Hudson Taylor in China.

Now, one hundred years later, I was holding in my hands the original letter from Hudson Taylor to John R. Mott dated May 17, 1900. As I held Taylor's letter, a chill ran down my spine as I sensed a glorious link with these giants of an earlier time. I wondered what Taylor would think of the developments in China today and its brave, vigorous church (much of which traces its roots back to his work). I mused how John R. Mott, one of the prime movers of student missions in his day, would rejoice in today's Urbana missions conferences and the radical, new youth missions movement. Then I remembered that Taylor and Mott do, in fact, see it all. They are part of heaven's "so great a cloud of witnesses" (Heb. 12:1).

Looking again at Hudson Taylor's letter I read:

**The evangelization of the world depends on
the full surrender of every Christian both at
home and abroad, so that the Holy Spirit may
be unhindered. Appeal to every reader to
unhesitatingly take this position.**[11]

Taylor's appeal to Mott's readers is the passionate plea I am now making to you. I don't want to be melodramatic, but you should know that as I write this I am literally on my knees, pleading with God as I plead with you. "O Lord, among every people and nation, glorify Your name! O God, use this book for Your high purposes and the eternal honor of Your Son! O Lord of the nations, lift the sights and the hopes of the one who is reading these words!"

Full surrender—take this position *now!* Let God take your precious life and use you for His purposes in ways beyond your highest hopes or dreams. When you are fully surrendered, God's Spirit is unhindered! Your life shifts from the natural to the supernatural. "By his mighty power at work within us, he is able to accomplish infinitely more than we would ever dare to ask or hope" (Eph. 3:20, NLT).

In the late 1940s an American newspaper reporter was stationed in the city of Shanghai, China. He watched from the balcony of his hotel one horrific night as Mao Tse-tung and troops loyal to Mao pillaged the city and burned much of it to the ground. The reporter watched as much as his stomach would allow. Finally, sickened by what he had just witnessed, he walked back into his room, sat at a little desk and wrote these words:

Tonight Shanghai is burning, and I am dying too,
But there's no death so real as the death inside of you.
Some men die by shrapnel and some go down in flames,
But most men die inch by inch playing little games.

Whatever else you do, don't die inch by inch, playing little games. Live for what matters! And what matters is the exaltation of the Son of God to the ends of the earth.

Afterword

A London cemetery seemed a conspicuous place to experience one of the most profound worship experiences of my life. But as I walked past the tombstones on that damp, cold day in January, my heart was getting white hot.

I suddenly found myself before the tombstone of John Bunyan. On one side of the stone is the effigy of a man struggling up a hill with a heavy burden on his back. On the other side, etched into the stone, the man is kneeling at the top of the hill, hands upraised toward a cross. The burden had been loosed and was rolling down the hillside. To anyone who has read Bunyan's immortal *The Pilgrim's Progress,* the testimony to Christ's saving power is unmistakable.

Walking a little farther, I saw the grave of Susanna Wesley, mother of John and Charles. I paused to thank God for this remarkable woman who instilled such a deep love for Christ in her sons. John would spark an awakening that would rescue a nation on the brink of spiritual ruin. Charles would exalt Christ to the masses through his grand hymns.

The missions addiction consumes me. The fire in me is no longer fueled by youth. Now it is fueled by truth.

Down one more row, I paused by the grave of John Rippon. One day, under the inspiration of the Spirit, this Baptist pastor wrote:

Let ev'ry kindred, ev'ry tribe, on this terrestrial ball,
To Him all majesty ascribe, and crown Him Lord of all.[1]

Then, as I turned the corner, I saw the grave of Isaac Watts. Watts gave to the church some of its most uplifting hymns. One day, a prophetic song swelled in Isaac Watts' heart. Taking his pen, he wrote:

Jesus shall reign where'er the sun
Does its successive journeys run;
His kingdom spread from shore to shore,
Till moons shall wax and wane no more.

Behold the islands with their kings,
And Europe her best tribute brings;
From north to south the princes meet,
To pay their homage at His feet.

Afterword

There Persia, glorious to behold,
There India shines in eastern gold;
And barb'rous nations at His word
Submit and bow and own their Lord.

To Him shall endless prayer be made,
And endless praises crown His head;
His name like sweet perfume shall rise
With ev'ry morning sacrifice.[2]

Watts was inspired by the multiple biblical promises that Jesus would rise to rule over all peoples. What makes this hymn even more prophetic is that it was written some seventy years before William Carey sailed for India, launching the modern missionary movement.

I'm writing this book in the springtime. Wild flowers adorn much of the rural landscape. The winter is past; ground that appeared dead and barren is bursting with color and life. I believe in the power of seeds.

Any romanticized view of missions has long since dissipated. I've seen too much tragedy in too many nations to harbor an unreal view of the present or the future. Yet as I enter my fifties, there is more heat—and more hope—in my heart than ever. The missions addiction consumes me. The fire in me is no longer fueled by youth. Now it is fueled by truth.

From Revelation 5 through 19, there are no less than seventeen scenes of majestic worship being given to Jesus Christ, often in the company of throngs of the redeemed from every tribe and nation. The history-long story of God's mission is brought to a glorious crescendo as heaven peels out praises to the reigning Lamb.

But this extravagant worship was preceded by a scene of agony in John's heart. Revelation 5 begins with the question: "Who is worthy to open the scroll and to loose its seals?" (v. 2). Is there anyone, anywhere, from any age who qualifies to tie up all the loose ends of time? Can anyone mete out perfect grace and also forever balance the scales of justice? Who among the great is mighty enough, or worthy enough, to write history's final chapter?

"All my life I've waited for this message."

A scan was made of the noble of all nations.

No one in heaven, on earth or under the earth was found worthy.

Knowing the implications, John wept convulsively. All of time and eternity hung suspended—creation itself was an unfinished symphony.

Then John's lament was interrupted by a news flash of victory. One had been found who is worthy! "Do not weep. Behold, the Lion of the tribe of Judah, the Root of David has prevailed to open the scroll and loose its seals (v. 5)."

Immediately John looks up from his tears and hears the cascading voices of multitudes worshiping the Worthy One:

You are worthy to take the scroll,
And to open its seals;
For You were slain,
And have redeemed us to God by Your blood
Out of every tribe and tongue and people and nation.
—REVELATION 5:9

The Worthy One will rise to rule over the peoples. The Worthy One will receive the reward of His sacrifice. Jesus shall reign.

* * * * *

Between now and Then our broken world waits, groaning for the crowning of the Worthy One. A few years ago I encountered one of the broken in Nagpur, India. The hunched-over woman who came to clean my room every day had been given the English name Sheila.

After befriending Sheila throughout the week, I wanted to share the gospel with her. As I told her of God's great love for her in Christ, tears filled her eyes. When I asked if she would like to receive the Gift, she immediately responded.

After we had prayed, Sheila looked at me with a newfound joy in her eyes. "Tonight, I will sleep in peace for the first time," she told me. "All my life I've waited for this message."

There are millions like Sheila around the world. They have waited all their lives for this message.

May you catch the missions addiction.

And may they wait no more.

Notes

CHAPTER ONE
HARVEST HOPE

1. For more information, see the Adopt-a-People Clearinghouse website: www.aapc.net.
2. William F. Arndt and F. Wilbur Gingrich, *A Greek-English Lexicon of the New Testament* and Walter Bauer, *Other Early Christian Literature* (Chicago: University of Chicago Press, 1957), 813.
3. "Rise Up, O Men of God" by William P. Merrill. Public domain.
4. 2 Corinthians 5:14–15.
5. Nicholas Wade, "Long-Held Beliefs Are Challenged By New Human Genome Analysis," *The New York Times* (February 12, 2001): A16.
6. Norman Barnes, e-mail correspondence, February 2, 2001.
7. Charles Fishman, "Change," *Fast Company* (April/May 1997): 66.
8. Matthew 13:24–30.
9. Grant McClung, *Globalbeliever.com* (Cleveland, TN: Pathway Press, 2000), 17.
10. Jim Reapsome, "The Perils of Change," *World Pulse* (August 18, 2000): 8.
11. A. W. Tozer, quoted by Helen Hossier, compiler, *The Quotable Christian* (Uhrichsville, OH: Barbour Publishing, 1998), 38.
12. "The Gospel of Jesus Christ: An Evangelical Celebration,"

The Committee on Evangelical Unity in the Gospel, 1999.

13. C. Peter Wagner, *Acts of the Holy Spirit* (Ventura, CA: Regal Books, 2000), 464.

14. This phrase is from the AD 2000 and Beyond Movement, www.ad2000.org.

15. Quoted in Stan Guthrie, *Missions in the Third Millennium* (n.p.: Paternoster Press, 2000), 145.

16. Quoted in J. Dudley Woodbury, "Muslims Tell: 'Why I Chose Jesus,'" *Mission Frontiers* (March 2001): 29.

17. See "The State of World Evangelization," www.missionfrontiers.org/newslinks/statewe.htm.

18. J. Dudley Woodbury, "Missiological Issues in the Encounter with Emerging Islam," *Missiology* 28, No. 1 (January 2000): 30.

19. Robert Stearns, *Prepare the Way* (Lake Mary, FL: Charisma House, 1999), 191.

20. Rick Wood, "The *JESUS* Film Makes Astounding Progress," *Mission Frontiers* (March 2001): 38.

21. "Mission Today," *Pulse* (August 20, 1999): 7.

22. "Measurable Progress," *Mission Frontiers* (June 2000): 28–29.

23. See "Status of Global Mission, 2001, in Context of 20th and 21st Centuries," *International Bulletin of Missionary Research,* January 2001, 25, David B. Barrett and Todd M. Johnson, "Annual Statistical Table on Global Mission: 2001

24. Justin Long, Reality-Check archives, www.egroups.com/messages/reality-check

25. "Milestones and the Future: An Interview with Paul Eshelman," *Mission Frontiers* (March 2001): 39.

26. Jack Hayford, "Journey to a.d. 2020," *Ministries Today* (September/October 2000): 23.

27. Ted Haggard, "The Fullness of Time," *Ministries Today* (September/October 2000): 25.

28. Quoted in John Piper, "The Supremacy of God in Missions Through Worship," *Into All the World,* 2001 edition, 8.

Chapter Two
Disaster Prevention

1. David J. Bosch, *Transforming Mission: Paradigm Shifts in Theology of Mission* (n.p.: Orbis Books, 1991), 496.

2. Quoted in Stan Guthrie, "Past Midnight," *Evangelical Missions Quarterly* (January 2000): 101.

3. Marilyn Lewis, "Overcoming Obstacles: The Broad Sweep of the African American and Missions," *Mission Frontiers* (April 2000): 28.

4. David Yonggi Cho, quoted in J. Lee Grady, *10 Lies the Church Tells Women* (Lake Mary, FL: Charisma House, 2000), 190.

5. Ibid., 203.

6. Don Richardson, *Eternity in Their Hearts* (Glendale, CA: Regal Books, 1984).

7. David Pawson, *The Road to Hell* (London: Hodder & Stoughton, 1992).

8. Charles Colson and Nancy Pearcey, *How Now Shall We Live?* (Wheaton, IL: Tyndale House Publishers, 1999), 196.

9. Quoted in Stan Guthrie, "Past Midnight," 102.

10. Pawson, *The Road to Hell*, 77.

11. Robertson McQuilkin, "Lost," *Perspectives on the World Christian Movement*, 3rd Edition, Ralph D. Winter and Steven C. Hawthorne, editors (Pasadena, CA: William Carey Library, 1999), 158–159.

12. Larry Stockstill, *Twenty-five Lines Around* (Baton Rouge, LA: Heartbeat Publishing, 1992), 2.

13. Ravi Zacharias, *Jesus Among Other Gods* (Nashville, TN: Word Publishing, 2000), 38.

14. Kenneth L. Woodward, "The Other Jesus," *Newsweek* (March 27, 2000): 60.

15. Zacharias, *Jesus Among Other Gods*, 143.

16. Ibid., 181.

17. John R. Mott, "The World Outlook and the World Mission" (June 28, 1936).

CHAPTER THREE
THE GLOBAL JESUS MOVEMENT

1. "The Happy Song" by Martin Smith. Copyright © 1994 Curious? Music UK, admin. by EMI Christian Publishing. All rights reserved. Used by permission.

2. Three independent sources estimated attendance at The Call DC to be more than 350,000. See Bill Broadway,

"Fervent Calls For a New Society," *The Washington Post* (September 3, 2000).

3. This phrase is from the AD 2000 and Beyond Movement, www.ad2000.org.

4. Toby McKeehan, quoted in "Elegy for a Jesus Freak," *Christianity Today* (December 6, 1999): 88.

5. Quoted by Brent Curtis with John Eldredge, *The Sacred Romance* (Nashville, TN: Thomas Nelson Publishers, 1997), 56.

6. "History Maker" by Martin Smith. Copyright © 1996 Curious? UK Music, admin. by EMI Christian Publishing. All rights reserved. Used by permission.

7. Winkey Pratney, *Fire on the Horizon* (Ventura, CA: Renew Books, 1999), 178.

8. Source: Terry Law, Heartland MissionFest, Tulsa, Oklahoma, February 20, 2001.

9. "The Year's Most Intriguing Findings," Barna Research Studies (December 12, 2000): www.barna.org.

10. Mark Curriden, "High court to hear religious club's case," *The Dallas Morning News* (February 28, 2001): 1A.

11. Pratney, *Fire on the Horizon*, 112, 78.

12. Philip Yancey, "Getting a Life," *Christianity Today* (October 23, 2000): 128.

13. See www.urbana.com.

14. John R. Mott, "The Responsibility of the Young People for the Evangelization of the World," Ralph D. Winter and Steven C. Hawthorne, *Perspectives on the World Christian Movement*, 3rd Edition (Pasadena, CA: William Carey Library, 1999), 322.

15. See John Dawson, *Healing America's Wounds* (Ventura, CA: Regal Books, 1994), 266–267.

CHAPTER FOUR
FAREWELL TO THE BALANCED LIFE

1. Ruth A. Tucker, *From Jerusalem to Irian Jaya* (Grand Rapids, MI: Zondervan Publishing House, 1983), 173.

2. T. E. Lawrence, *Seven Pillars of Wisdom: A Triumph* (n.p.: Anchor, 1935, 1991).

3. Jonah 4:3

4. Jonah 4:2, NIV

Notes

5. Dietrich Bonhoeffer, *The Cost of Discipleship* (New York: Macmillan Books, 1970), 196.

6. "Mario Murillo on Revival," *Twenty Lessons Learned While Walking With God* (Lake Mary, FL: Strang Communications, 1996), 15.

7. Ralph D. Winter, "Introduction," *Finishing the Task*, compiled by John E. Kyle (Ventura, CA: Regal Books, 1987), 12.

8. Winston Churchill, quoted in John Bartlett, editor, *Familiar Quotations* (Boston, MA: Little, Brown and Company, 1968), 925.

9. Stockstill, *Twenty-five Lines Around*, 1–2.

10. Amy Carmichael, quoted in Elisabeth Elliot, *A Chance to Die* (Grand Rapids, MI: Fleming H. Revell Company, 1987), 221.

11. Jim Elliot, quoted in Elisabeth Elliot, *Shadow of the Almighty* (New York: Harper & Brothers, 1958), 249.

CHAPTER FIVE
TRIPLE THREAT IN THE HEAVENLIES

1. Mark Geppart, *Every Place Your Foot Shall Tread* (Vail, CO: SOAR Publishers, 1999), 210–211.

2. Steve Hawthorne and Graham Kendrick, *Prayerwalking* (Lake Mary, FL: Charisma House, 1993), 189–190.

3. Ibid., 190.

4. David Bryant, "The Levites: Their Strategy and Ours," *Finishing the Task*, 175.

5. Anne Graham Lotz, *The Vision of His Glory* (Nashville, TN: Word Publishing, 1997), 130–131.

6. C. Peter Wagner, "Looking Back to Surge Ahead," *Global Prayer News* (July/September 2000): 12.

7. "C. Peter Wagner Calls for 'Spiritual House Cleaning,'" *Charisma* (June 2001): 40.

8. See Steven C. Hawthorne, "The Story of His Glory," *Perspectives on the World Christian Movement*, 3rd Edition (Pasadena, CA: William Carey Library, 1999), 34.

9. Patrick Johnstone, *Operation World* (Grand Rapids, MI: Zondervan Publishing House, 1993). A new edition is scheduled for release next year.

10. Ed Silvoso, *Prayer Evangelism* (Ventura, CA: Regal Books, 2000), 37.

11. Wagner, *Acts of the Holy Spirit*, 422.

12. C. Peter Wagner, *Lighting the World* (Ventura, CA: Regal Books, 1995), 41.

13. *Prepare the Way*, 108.

14. George Otis, Jr., *Informed Intercession* (Ventura, CA: Renew Books, 1999), 82.

15. Wagner, *Acts of the Holy Spirit*, 22.

16. Frank Damazio, *Crossing Rivers, Taking Cities* (Ventura, CA: Regal Books, 1999), 271.

17. See Chuck Lowe, *Territorial Spirits and World Evangelization?* (Mentor Publications) and John Paul Jackson, *Needless Casualties of War* (Streams Publications).

18. Otis, *Informed Intercession*, 222.

19. T. L. Osborn, *The Message That Works* (Tulsa, OK: OSFO Books, 1997), 273.

20. Ibid., 316.

21. Guthrie, *Missions in the New Millennium*, 82–83.

22. Silvoso, *Prayer Evangelism*, 87.

23. John Piper, *God's Passion for His Glory* (Wheaton, IL: Crossway Books, 1998), 42.

24. Sosene Leau, *Called to Honor Him* (Tampa, FL: CultureCom Press, 1997), 21.

25. "O for a Thousand Tongues to Sing" by Charles Wesley. Public domain.

26. Quoted by Tim Sheppard, "Great Stories," *Ministry Spotlight*, Volume 7, Issue 28 (October/December 2000): 17.

27. Dutch Sheets, *Intercessory Prayer* (Ventura, CA: Regal Books, 1996), 231.

28. Mike Bickle, quoted by Ken Walker, "The Rise of Prophetic Worship," *Ministries Today* (September/October 2000): 34.

29. Mike Bickle, quoted in "Gathered around His Throne," *Renewal* 26 (November 2000).

30. Brent Curtis and John Eldredge, *The Sacred Romance* (Nashville, TN: Thomas Nelson Publishers, 1997), 45.

31. Steve Fry, from an upcoming book to be published by Multnomah Press.

Notes

32. Floyd McClung, "Apostolic Passion," *Perspectives on the World Christian Movement,* Ralph D. Winter, Steven C. Hawthorne, editors (Pasadena, CA: William Carey Library, 1999), 185.

CHAPTER SIX
THE WHOLE WORLD IS WATCHING

1. Quoted by Michael L. Brown, *Revolution!* (Ventura, CA: Renew Books, 2000), 166.

2. Robert E. Coleman, *The Great Commission Lifestyle* (Grand Rapids, MI: Fleming H. Revell, 1992), 97.

3. Brown, *Revolution!,* 40.

4. Quoted in Stan Guthrie, "Past Midnight," 101.

5. Our accountability questions are: Since we last met . . .

   1) Have you had a daily time with the Lord?

   2) Have you been above reproach in all your financial dealings?

   3) Have you fulfilled the mandate of your calling?

   4) Have you been with a woman in a way that could be perceived as inappropriate?

   5) Have you sought out any explicit or pornographic material?

   6) How is your marriage?

   7) Have you just lied?

6. "Trust and Obey" by John H. Sammis. Public domain.

7. J. Christy Wilson, Jr., "What Can We Learn from the Student Volunteer Movement?" *Finishing the Task,* 60.

8. Pratney, *Fire on the Horizon,* 77.

9. Antinomianism literally means "against law." It is an ancient heresy asserting that grace cancels any need for moral law. Paul was slanderously accused of propagating this teaching because of his strong emphasis on grace and the finished work of Christ as the sole means of salvation. Concerning those who accused him of promoting antino-mianism, Paul said, "Their condemnation is deserved" (Rom. 3:8, NIV).

10. Statistic quoted by Josh McDowell in a personal conversation with him, April 14, 2000.

11. Jack Hayford, "Don't Marriage Vows Matter Anymore?" *Charisma* (February 2001): 60.

12. Andrew Murray, *Humility* (New Kensington, PA: Whitaker House, 1982), 90.
13. Paul E. Billheimer, *Destined for the Throne* (Fort Washington, PA: Christian Literature Crusade, 1975), 98.
14. Ibid., 21–22.
15. Oswald Chambers, *My Utmost for His Highest* (New York: Dodd, Mead & Company, 1935), 91.
16. Herbert J. Kane, *Wanted: World Christians* (Grand Rapids, MI: Baker Book House, 1986).
17. Herbert J. Kane, "Every Christian a World Christian," *The Christian World Mission Today and Tomorrow* (Grand Rapids, MI: Baker Book House, 1981), 57–69.
18. Chambers, *My Utmost for His Highest*, 56.
19. Elliot, *Shadow of the Almighty*, 132.
20. Paul Lee Tan, editor, *Encyclopedia of 7700 Illustrations* (n.c.: Assurance Books, 1977), 1367.

CHAPTER SEVEN
THE INCREDIBLE SHRINKING GIANT

1. George Barna and Mark Hatch, *Boiling Point* (Ventura, CA: Regal Books, 2001), 311.
2. Andrew Walls, "The Growth of the Christian Church," Peter Brierley and Heather Wraight, editors, *Atlas of World Christianity* (Nashville, TN: Thomas Nelson Publishers, 1998), 11.
3. See Genesis 12:1–3.
4. *Insight for Living* broadcast. Date unknown.
5. Ron Rose, "Christianity growth falls flat in U.S.," *The Dallas/Fort Worth Heritage*, Vol. 8 No. 10 (May 2000): 1.
6. See www.missionamerica.org.
7. Colson and Pearcey, *How Now Shall We Live?* 31.
8. Barna and Hatch, *Boiling Point*, 239.
9. Paul E. Pierson and A. Scott Moreau, editors, *Evangelical Dictionary of World Missions* (Grand Rapids, MI: Baker Books, 2000), 986.
10. Barna and Hatch, *Boiling Point*, 220.
11. Ibid., 221.
12. Ibid., 237.
13. Leonard Sweet, *Soul Tsunami* (Grand Rapids, MI: Zondervan Publishing House, 1999), 51.

Notes

14. C. Peter Wagner, general editor, *The New Apostolic Churches* (Ventura, CA: Regal Books, 1998), 20.
15. Ephesians 4:11–12.
16. The Greek word that is often translated as *Gentiles* is *ta ethne*, literally "the ethnicities" or "the peoples."
17. Roland Allen, *Missionary Methods: St. Paul's or Ours?* (Grand Rapids, MI: Wm. B. Eerdmans Publishing, 1962), 75.
18. C. Peter Wagner, *Churchquake!* (Ventura, CA: Regal Books, 1999), 4.
19. Dale Galloway, "Outreach through Small Groups," *Strategies for Today's Leader*, Vol. 32, No. 2 (Spring 1999): 1–4.
20. Elmer Towns in Wagner, *The New Apostolic Churches*, 9.
21. C. Peter Wagner, *Apostles of the City* (Colorado Springs, CO: Wagner Publications, 2000), 50.
22. William F. Arndt and F. Wilbur Gingrich, *A Greek-English Lexicon of the New Testament and Other Early Christian Literature* (Chicago, IL: University of Chicago Press, 1957), 690.
23. The Millennial Manifesto: Covenanting Together for the 21st Century.
24. Adrienne S. Gaines, "The Apology That Shook a Continent," *Charisma* (March 2000): 77–85.
25. John Dawson, *What Christians Should Know About Reconciliation* (Ventura, CA: International Reconciliation Coalition, 1998), 28.
26. Silvoso, *Prayer Evangelism*, 127.
27. James F. Engel and William A. Dyrness, *Changing the Mind of Missions* (Downers Grove, IL: InterVarsity Press, 2000), 125.
28. Larry Reesor, "The Local Church's Role in Missions," *Mission Frontiers* (June 2000): 45.
29. See Patrick Johnstone, *The Church Is Bigger Than You Think* (n.p.: Christian Focus Publications, 1998).
30. George Verwer, *Out of the Comfort Zone* (Minneapolis, MN: Bethany House, 2000), 23.
31. "World Evangelism in the 21st Century," *Charisma* (December 1999): 51.
32. See David Shibley, "Healthy Church Vision," *Ministries Today* (September/October 2000): 47.
33. Excellent resources for helping local churches link with unreached peoples are available from The Caleb Project

(www.calebproject.org) and Adopt-a-People Clearinghouse
(www.aapc.net).

34. Six thousand people die every day in sub-Sahara Africa of
symptoms related to AIDS. See Adrienne S. Gaines, "A
Continent in Crisis," *Charisma* (March 2001): 80–90.

CHAPTER EIGHT
HIDDEN HEROES

1. Bruce Wilkinson, *The Prayer of Jabez* (Sisters, OR:
Multnomah Publishers, 2000), 6.

2. See Robertson McQuilkin, "Stop Sending Money!"
Christianity Today (March 1, 1999) and the response by Bob
Finley, "Send Dollars and Sense," *Christianity Today*
(October 4, 1999).

3. Melvin Hodges, *The Indigenous Church* (Springfield, MO:
Gospel Publishing House, 1953, 1976), 14.

4. Wagner, *Acts of the Holy Spirit*, 471.

5. National Pastors Prayer Network, February 28, 2001.

6. Philip Jenkins, "The changing face of Christianity," *The
Dallas Morning News* (April 8, 2000): 3G.

7. Ken Macharg, "Brazil's Surging Spirituality," *Christianity
Today* (December 4, 2000): 72.

8. J. Lee Grady, "An Abnormal Gospel" *Charisma* (March
2001): 6.

9. Grant McClung, "The Pentecostal 'Trunk' Must Learn from
Its 'Branches,'" *Evangelical Missions Quarterly* (January 1993):
38.

10. David Bryant, *The Hope at Hand* (Grand Rapids, MI: Baker,
1995), 223.

11. Howard Foltz, *Triumph: Mission Renewal for the Local Church*
(Joplin, MO: Messenger Books, 1994), 167.

12. Rigoberro Galvez, quoted by Kenneth D. MacHarg, "Word
and Spirit Together," *Christianity Today* (October 23, 2000): 26.

13. C. Peter Wagner, *Blazing the Way* (Ventura, CA: Regal
Books, 1995), 48.

14. Jonathan David, *Apostolic Strategies Affecting Nations* (Johor,
Malaysia: 1999), 114.

15. Deann Alford, "Koreans aim to win the world," *World Pulse*
(August 4, 2000): 1.

Notes

16. John Eckhardt, *Moving in the Apostolic* (Ventura, CA: Regal Books, 1999), 17.
17. Steve Saint, "Looking at Missions from Their Side, Not Ours," 36.
18. *Brigada Today,* March 16, 2001.
19. C. Peter Wagner, "Prayer and the Order of the Church," *Global Prayer News* (April–June 2000): 12.

Chapter Nine
Siege on the Saints

1. *InterSeed,* Vol. 8, No. 1, (1997).
2. "Nigerian Pastor Once Persecuted Christians, But Now Lives for Christ," *Charisma* (March 2001): 40–41.
3. "What Beijing Doesn't Want Us to Know," *Charisma* (October 2000): 64.
4. CNN.com/World, March 19, 2001.
5. Personal correspondence with Gary Russell, China Harvest, February 27, 2001.
6. Ralph Kinney Bennett, "The Global War on Christians," *Reader's Digest* (August 1997): 54.
7. Joseph D'Sousa, "InterView," *World Pulse* (December 15, 2000): 5.
8. Peter Kuzmic, quoted by John R. W. Stott, "Which Jesus are we talking about now?" *The Dallas Morning News* (March 17, 2001): 4G.
9. Rachel Scott, quoted by Wendy Murray Zoba, "Do You Believe in God? Columbine and the stirring of America's soul," *Christianity Today* (October 4, 1999): 40.
10. "Noon in the Garden of Good and Evil," *Time* (May 17, 1999): 54.
11. Winkey Pratney, *Fire on the Horizon,* 113.
12. "Missionaries facing world of new perils," *Chicago Tribune* (April 28, 2001): 1, 19.
13. Hope Flinchbaugh, "Christians in the Line of Fire," *Charisma* (October 1999): 75.
14. Summary Statement, Consultation on Mission Language and Metaphors.
15. Colson and Pearcy, *How Now Shall We Live?,* 299.

16. Quoted by Kim A. Lawton, "Killed in the Line of Duty," *Charisma* (October 1995): 59.

17. Rebecca Rodriguez, "Shootings at Wedgwood Baptist Church: One Year Later," *Fort Worth Star Telegram* (September 15, 2000): 29A.

18. Laurie Fox, "Prophets of Hope: Three churches still building on tragedies," *The Dallas Morning News* (September 9, 2000): 1G.

19. Winkey Pratney, *Fire on the Horizon*, 71.

20. James Russell Lowell, "Once to Every Man and Nation" (1845).

CHAPTER 10
FINISH LINE IN SIGHT!

1. Revelation 11:15

2. Guthrie, *Missions in the Third Millennium*, 193.

3. Malcolm Gladwell, *The Tipping Point* (Boston, MA: Little, Brown and Company, 2000), 12.

4. See chapter five for a treatment of the relation of intercessory travail to the spiritual birth of peoples.

5. Chambers, *My Utmost for His Highest*, 58.

6. From a personal conversation with Robert Abramson, missionary to Fiji, June, 1997.

7. From a personal conversation and correspondence with Kirk DeVenney, October 17, 2000.

8. John Piper, *Let the Nations Be Glad!* (Grand Rapids, MI: Baker Book House, 1993), 228.

9. Tetsanao Yamamori, quoted by Verwer, *Out of the Comfort Zone*, 41.

10. Chambers, *My Utmost for His Highest*, 362.

11. John R. Mott papers, Series I, Day Missions Library, Yale Divinity School.

AFTERWORD

1. "All Hail the Power of Jesus' Name," verse 3 by John Rippon. Public domain.

2. "Jesus Shall Reign" by Isaac Watts. Public domain.

Index

Index

Index

EQUIPPING FRONTLINE SHEPHERDS FOR WORLD HARVEST

On the front lines of the church's advance around the world stand God's hidden heroes—the native pastors, evangelists and church leaders who willingly sacrifice everything to preach the gospel and establish churches among the unreached. Often these pastoral leaders face incredible opposition.

In 1990 David Shibley founded Global Advance to meet the desperate need to equip these frontline shepherds. Through Frontline Shepherds Conferences and Global Advance Institutes, these hidden heroes receive effective training, relevant ministry resources and much needed encouragement and fellowship. For many, it is the only ministry training they have ever received. They go back into the battle with a vision in their hearts and tools in their hands.

Since 1990 Global Advance has provided on-site training for some 200,000 pastoral leaders in fifty-two nations. You are invited to share the vision of equipping one million of these hidden heroes to reach their nations and unreached peoples for Jesus Christ. You can help fulfill the Great Commission by partnering with Global Advance to equip frontline shepherds for world harvest. Your prayers and financial support will make a world of difference in the lives of heaven's hidden heroes.

To receive your free subscription to the *Global Advance Update,* or for more information about Global Advance's ministry to the church's hidden heroes, contact:

GLOBAL ADVANCE
P. O. Box 742077
Dallas, Texas 75374-2077
Phone: (972) 771-9042
Website: www.globaladvance.org